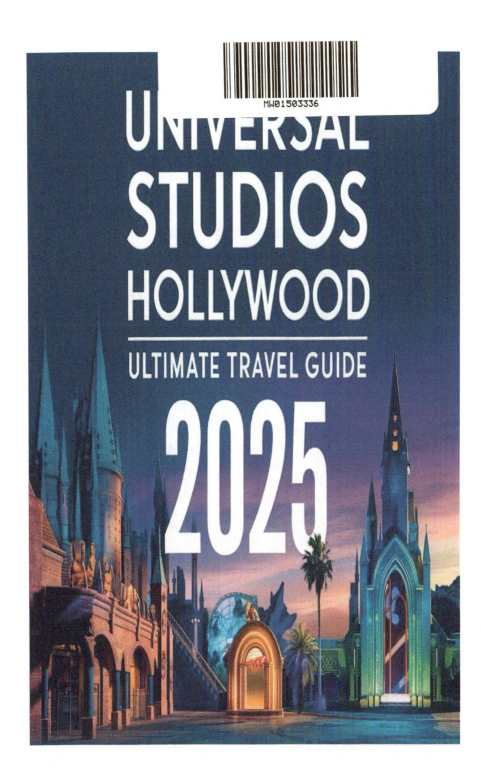

UNIVERSAL STUDIOS HOLLYWOOD

ULTIMATE TRAVEL GUIDE

2025

Copyright ©

Universal Fan Fest Nights (April 25–May 18, 2025)
Get ready for an unforgettable after-hours experience at **Universal Fan Fest Nights,** a brand-new event that blends the excitement of sci-fi, fantasy, gaming, and anime into one spectacular celebration. Picture a mash-up of **Halloween Horror Nights** and a vibrant pop culture convention, complete with themed attractions, interactive experiences, and surprises for fans of all genres.

Unnamed Summer Event (June 14–August 10, 2025)
Summer 2025 is heating up at Universal Studios Hollywood with a thrilling new event set to take center stage. While the details are still under wraps, you can expect an epic celebration filled with entertainment, excitement, and unforgettable memories. Mark your calendar and stay tuned—this summer extravaganza is one you won't want to miss!

Halloween Horror Nights (September 4–November 2, 2025)
Prepare for another season of chills, thrills, and spine-tingling scares as **Halloween Horror Nights** returns to Universal Studios Hollywood! From immersive haunted houses to terrifying scare zones and eerie live entertainment, this iconic event is a must-see for fans of horror and adrenaline-pumping fun. If you've never experienced it, 2025 is the perfect time to dive into the haunting magic of one of the most celebrated Halloween events in the world.

Holidays at Universal Studios Hollywood (November–December 2025)
Celebrate the magic of the holiday season at Universal Studios Hollywood, where beloved worlds come alive with festive cheer! Experience **Christmas in The Wizarding World of Harry Potter,** complete with dazzling lights, enchanting decorations, and seasonal treats. Don't forget to visit **Grinchmas,** where the mischievous Grinch takes center stage with his heartwarming holiday antics.

Table of Contents

Introduction
What's New in 2025
Planning Your Trip
Getting There
Directions from Los Angeles and Surrounding Areas
Parking Options and Tips
Public Transportation and Shuttle Services
Tickets and Packages
Types of Tickets
Annual Passes
Seasonal Promotions and Discounts
Booking Online vs. At the Gate
Navigating the Park
Park Layout: Upper Lot and Lower Lot
Understanding Wait Times and Crowd Flow
The Universal Studios App
Attractions and Rides
Upper Lot
The Wizarding World of Harry Potter
Despicable Me: Minion Mayhem
The Simpsons Ride
Secret Life of Pets: Off the Leash

Lower Lot:
Jurassic World: The Ride
Transformers: The Ride 3D
Revenge of the Mummy: The Ride
Studio Tour:
Behind the Scenes: Classic and Modern Film Sets
King Kong 360 3D and Fast & Furious Supercharged
Live Shows and Entertainment
WaterWorld: A Live Sea War Spectacular
Special Effects Show
Character Meet-and-Greets
Dining and Snacks
Dining Guide by Area: Quick Bites vs. Sit-Down Meals
Must-Try Themed Food: Butterbeer, Minion Treats, and More
Vegetarian, Vegan, and Gluten-Free Options
Shopping and Souvenirs
Top Souvenir Shops: From Harry Potter Wands to Minion Plushies
Exclusive Merchandise
Shopping Tips to Save Money

Tips for Families
Visiting with Kids: Rides and Activities for All Ages
Baby Care Centers and Kid-Friendly Amenities
Managing Strollers and Baby Gear
Seasonal Events
Halloween Horror Nights
Lunar New Year Celebrations
Grinchmas and Winter Wonderland
Other Limited-Time Experiences in 2025
Accessibility and Inclusivity
Wheelchair Accessibility Across the Park
Services for Guests with Hearing or Visual Impairments
Sensory-Friendly Attractions and Quiet Zones
Best Times to Visit
Crowd Patterns Throughout the Year
Weather Guide by Season
Avoiding Long Lines
Nearby Accommodations
On-Site Hotel Options
Recommended Hotels Near Universal Studios
Transportation Options from Hotels

Exploring Beyond the Park
Universal CityWalk: Shopping, Dining, and Entertainment
Nearby Los Angeles Attractions to Pair with Your Visit
Budgeting Your Visit
Daily Expense Breakdown
Money-Saving Tips
Balancing Fun and Affordability
Insider Tips and Hacks
Best Seats for Shows and Attractions
Maximizing the Universal Express Pass
Secrets Only Locals Know
Final Checklist
What to Pack for a Day at the Park
Key Things to Know Before You Go
Tips for a Memorable Experience
Frequently Asked Questions (FAQs)
Top Questions Visitors Ask
Common Pitfalls and How to Avoid Them
Conclusion
Making the Most of Universal Studios Hollywood in 2025

INTRODUCTION

Welcome to **Universal Studios Hollywood**, the entertainment capital of Los Angeles! Nestled in the heart of the San Fernando Valley, this world-famous theme park and working film studio is a must-visit destination for movie lovers, thrill-seekers, and families alike. Whether you're a lifelong fan of Hollywood magic or visiting for the very first time, Universal Studios Hollywood offers an unforgettable blend of iconic attractions, blockbuster-themed rides, live entertainment, and behind-the-scenes glimpses into the film industry.

A Park Like No Other

Universal Studios Hollywood is more than just a theme park; it's where the magic of movies comes to life. Known for its unique combination of exhilarating rides and authentic movie-making experiences, the park brings beloved films and TV shows to vivid reality. From exploring the corridors of Hogwarts at **The Wizarding World of Harry Potter** to escaping dinosaurs on **Jurassic World: The Ride**, there's something for everyone.

What's New in 2025

This year, the park continues to elevate the visitor experience with exciting updates and additions:

- **New Attractions:** Get ready to experience a brand-new ride (details to be revealed soon!), rumored to immerse guests in another Hollywood classic.
- **Improved Technology:** Enhanced mobile app features for shorter wait times, personalized itineraries, and real-time updates.
- **Special Events:** More immersive seasonal events like Halloween Horror Nights and Grinchmas.

The Perfect Blend of Fun and Film

Universal Studios Hollywood is unique in being both a thrilling theme park and an active film studio. You'll find yourself walking through movie sets, witnessing real productions, and stepping into the worlds of your favorite films and TV shows. The famous **Studio Tour** offers an unparalleled peek behind the curtain, featuring classics like the **Bates Motel**, **Jaws**, and cutting-edge attractions like **King Kong 360 3D**.

A Global Destination

With visitors from around the world, Universal Studios Hollywood is a cultural melting pot where everyone can enjoy the magic of Hollywood. Whether you're traveling solo, with friends, or as a family, the park's diverse offerings make it an all-inclusive destination.

This guide is your ultimate companion to navigating the park in 2025, helping you plan your day, discover hidden gems, and maximize every moment. So, grab your map, lace up your walking shoes, and prepare to make memories that will last a lifetime. Welcome to **Universal Studios Hollywood**—your adventure starts now!

Planning Your Trip
Why This Guide is Essential

Visiting Universal Studios Hollywood is more than just a day at a theme park—it's stepping into the world of your favorite movies, shows, and unforgettable experiences. But with so much to see, do, and enjoy, a well-thought-out plan can mean the difference between a magical adventure and a stressful, overwhelming day. That's where this guide comes in. It's not just a map of attractions or a list of restaurants—it's your personal assistant, travel planner, and insider companion, designed to make your trip seamless, stress-free, and spectacular.

Maximize Your Time

Universal Studios Hollywood is a park of endless possibilities, but let's face it: lines can be long, and time is precious. This guide helps you:

- **Prioritize Must-See Attractions:** We break down the park's rides, shows, and experiences so you know what's worth your time. Whether you're a Potterhead, a thrill-seeker, or traveling with little ones, we'll help you focus on what matters most to you.
- **Navigate Like a Pro:** From the sprawling Upper Lot to the action-packed Lower Lot, we'll show you how to move efficiently between attractions without wasting a second.

Insider Tips and Secrets

Every great trip includes a little insider knowledge, and that's exactly what this guide provides:

- **Beat the Crowds:** Discover the best times to visit each attraction and how to avoid peak wait times.
- **Hidden Gems:** We'll show you off-the-radar spots and lesser-known experiences that most visitors miss, like secret photo ops or underrated dining options.
- **Pro Tips for Families:** Whether you're bringing toddlers or teenagers, this guide includes practical advice to make the day enjoyable for everyone.

Save Money Without Missing Out

Universal Studios Hollywood can be expensive, but that doesn't mean you need to break the bank. In this guide, you'll find:

- The best ways to snag discounts on tickets and dining.
- Affordable souvenir options that won't blow your budget.
- Hacks for getting the most out of the **Universal Express Pass** or other add-ons.

Plan for Special Events

From the spine-tingling thrills of **Halloween Horror Nights** to the whimsical magic of **Grinchmas**, Universal Studios Hollywood transforms with the seasons. This guide keeps you updated on all the special events, limited-time attractions, and seasonal food offerings so you can plan accordingly.

Stress-Free Planning for Every Visitor

Whether you're a solo traveler, a couple on a romantic getaway, or a family navigating stroller-friendly paths, this guide is tailored to meet your needs. It includes:

- Accessibility tips for guests with disabilities.
- Dining options for every dietary preference.
- Packing checklists and tips for unpredictable California weather.

Why This Guide is Different

Unlike generic travel advice, this guide is written with 2025 in mind—covering all the latest updates, trends, and must-know details. From brand-new rides to fresh dining options, it's your ultimate resource for staying ahead of the curve.

Your adventure at Universal Studios Hollywood should be magical, exciting, and unforgettable. With this guide, you'll have everything you need to make the most of your trip—every laugh, scream, and "wow" moment included.

CHAPTER 1

Getting There

Directions from Los Angeles and Surrounding Areas Universal Studios Hollywood, located at **100 Universal City Plaza, Universal City, CA 91608**, is conveniently situated in the heart of the greater Los Angeles area, making it accessible from many nearby cities and neighborhoods. Here's your ultimate guide to getting to the park, no matter where you're coming from.

From Downtown Los Angeles (10 miles, ~20 minutes by car)
- **By Car:**
  - Take **US-101 North (Hollywood Freeway)** toward Hollywood.
  - Exit at **Universal Studios Boulevard** and follow the signs to the park entrance.
  - Parking is available on-site, with multiple options (more on that later).

By Public Transportation:
  - Take the **Metro Red Line** subway from Union Station to **Universal City/Studio City Station** (approximately 15 minutes).
  - From there, hop on the **Universal Studios Shuttle**, which provides free transportation from the station to the park's main entrance (less than 5 minutes).

From Hollywood (5 miles, ~10 minutes by car)
- **By Car:**
  - Take **US-101 North** toward Ventura.

- Exit at **Universal Studios Boulevard** and follow the signs to the park.

By Public Transportation:
- Board the **Metro Red Line** at the Hollywood/Highland Station.
- Get off at **Universal City/Studio City Station** and take the complimentary shuttle.

From Los Angeles International Airport (LAX) (25 miles, ~40-60 minutes by car)
- **By Car:**
  - Take **I-405 North** toward Santa Monica.
  - Merge onto **US-101 South** toward Los Angeles.
  - Exit at **Universal Studios Boulevard**.

By Public Transportation:
- Take the **FlyAway Bus** from LAX to **Union Station** in Downtown Los Angeles.
- Transfer to the **Metro Red Line** subway, heading toward **North Hollywood**.
- Exit at **Universal City/Studio City Station** and take the free shuttle.

From Santa Monica (20 miles, ~30-45 minutes by car)
- **By Car:**
  1. Take **I-10 East** toward Los Angeles.
  2. Merge onto **I-405 North** and then onto **US-101 South**.
  3. Exit at **Universal Studios Boulevard**.
- **By Public Transportation:**
  1. Take the **Big Blue Bus Line 10** to Downtown Los Angeles.
  2. Transfer to the **Metro Red Line** at Union Station.

3. Exit at **Universal City/Studio City Station** and board the shuttle.

From Pasadena (15 miles, ~20-30 minutes by car)
- **By Car:**
  - Take **CA-134 West** toward Burbank.
  - Merge onto **US-101 South** toward Los Angeles.
  - Exit at **Universal Studios Boulevard**.
- **By Public Transportation:**
  - Board the **Metro Gold Line** toward Downtown Los Angeles.
  - Transfer to the **Metro Red Line** at Union Station.
  - Exit at **Universal City/Studio City Station** and use the shuttle service.

From Anaheim (Disneyland Area) (40 miles, ~1-1.5 hours by car)
- **By Car:**
  - Take **I-5 North** toward Los Angeles.
  - Merge onto **US-101 North** and exit at **Universal Studios Boulevard**.
- **By Public Transportation:**
  - Take an **Amtrak or Metrolink Train** from Anaheim to Union Station in Los Angeles.
  - Transfer to the **Metro Red Line** subway.
  - Exit at **Universal City/Studio City Station** and board the shuttle.

From Burbank (7 miles, ~15 minutes by car)
- **By Car:**
  - Take **CA-134 East** toward Glendale.
  - Merge onto **US-101 South** toward Los Angeles.
  - Exit at **Universal Studios Boulevard**.

- **By Public Transportation:**
  - Take a **Metrolink Train** from Burbank to Union Station.
  - Transfer to the **Metro Red Line** subway.
  - Exit at **Universal City/Studio City Station** and use the shuttle service.

Navigating Traffic and Parking
- **Traffic Tips:**
  Los Angeles is infamous for its traffic, so plan to travel during off-peak hours (before 7 AM or after 7 PM). Use navigation apps like Waze or Google Maps for real-time updates on road conditions.
- **Parking Options:**
  1. **General Parking:** Best for budget-conscious travelers, though a short walk from the entrance is required.
  2. **Preferred Parking:** Closer to the park entrance for added convenience.
  3. **Front Gate Parking:** The most expensive option but ideal for those who want premium convenience.
  4. **Valet Parking:** Perfect for those looking for the fastest and easiest parking experience.

With these detailed directions and options, your journey to Universal Studios Hollywood will be as smooth as possible. Whether you're driving, using public transit, or coming from across town, getting there is part of the adventure!

Parking Options and Tips at Universal Studios Hollywood

Parking at Universal Studios Hollywood is straightforward, but understanding your options can save you time, money, and stress. The park offers several parking tiers tailored to different needs, whether you're looking for convenience, affordability, or VIP treatment. This guide breaks down each option and provides insider tips to make your parking experience hassle-free.

Parking Options
1. General Parking
- **Cost:** ~$30-$40 (varies by season and time of day).
- **Location:** The furthest from the park entrance, typically in the lower levels of the parking structure.
- **Ideal For:** Budget-conscious visitors who don't mind a 10-15 minute walk to the park entrance.
- **Additional Info:** Complimentary trams may be available during peak times to shuttle guests from the parking lot to the main entrance.

2. Preferred Parking
- **Cost:** ~$50-$70.
- **Location:** Closer to the entrance than general parking, typically on the upper levels of the parking structure or in designated areas.
- **Ideal For:** Visitors who want to reduce walking time without splurging on premium options.
- **Additional Info:** This option is particularly useful for families with strollers or guests who plan to leave and return during the day.

3. Front Gate Parking
- **Cost:** ~$70-$100.
- **Location:** Directly in front of the main park entrance.

- **Ideal For:** Guests who value convenience and want the shortest possible walk to the park entrance.
- **Additional Info:** Front Gate Parking is limited, so it's best to arrive early to secure a spot.

4. Valet Parking
- **Cost:** ~$100-$120.
- **Location:** The closest parking option, with attendants parking and retrieving your vehicle for you.
- **Ideal For:** Visitors who prioritize luxury, convenience, or are on a tight schedule.
- **Additional Info:** Valet service is excellent for special occasions or if you're running late and want to maximize park time.

5. EV Charging Stations
- **Cost:** Standard parking fee + EV charging fee.
- **Location:** Found in select areas of the parking structures.
- **Ideal For:** Electric vehicle owners who need to charge while visiting the park.
- **Additional Info:** Charging stations are limited, so plan to arrive early if you need to charge your car.

6. Accessible Parking
- **Cost:** Same as General or Preferred Parking.
- **Location:** Closer to elevators and walkways for guests with disabilities.
- **Ideal For:** Guests with valid disabled parking placards or license plates.
- **Additional Info:** Accessible spaces are available in all parking tiers. Early arrival is recommended to secure a spot.

Insider Tips for Parking at Universal Studios Hollywood
1. **Arrive Early**
   o Parking lots open approximately an hour before the park. Arriving early not only ensures better parking

spots but also allows you to be one of the first in line for attractions.

2. **Consider Parking After 5 PM**
   o If you're visiting for **CityWalk** or evening events, parking rates are often discounted after 5 PM. This is a great option for dining, shopping, or attending seasonal events like Halloween Horror Nights.

3. **Use the Universal Studios App**
   o The app provides real-time updates on parking availability and directions to the best parking structure for your needs.

4. **Know Your Lot**
   o Universal Studios has multiple parking structures, including the Jurassic Parking Garage, Frankenstein Garage, and King Kong Garage. Make note of your structure and level to avoid confusion when returning to your car. Take a photo of the parking marker for reference.

5. **Avoid Weekend and Holiday Crowds**
   o Parking lots fill up quickly on weekends and holidays. Aim for weekdays or non-peak seasons for a smoother parking experience.

6. **Combine Parking with Dining**
   o If you're visiting **CityWalk** and spending at least $25 at participating restaurants or shops, you may be eligible for parking validation to reduce your fee. Check with the merchant for details.

7. **Bring Cash/Card for Payment**
   o Parking fees can be paid via cash or credit/debit card. Ensure you have payment ready to speed up the process at the gates.

8. **Consider Ride-Share for Convenience**
    o If parking seems overwhelming or you're staying at a nearby hotel, using a ride-share service like Uber or Lyft can eliminate the hassle of parking altogether. Designated drop-off and pick-up zones are located near the park entrance.
9. **Plan for Exit Traffic**
    o Exiting the parking structures after the park closes can take time, especially during peak seasons or after major events. To avoid delays, consider staying for a late dinner at CityWalk or leaving slightly before closing time.
10. **Use Preferred or Front Gate for Quick Departures**
    o If you plan to leave mid-day or early evening, investing in Preferred or Front Gate parking can save significant time when exiting the park.

FAQs About Parking at Universal Studios Hollywood
- **Q: Can I leave and return with the same parking ticket?**
  A: Yes, re-entry is permitted on the same day with a valid parking receipt. Make sure to keep your receipt!
- **Q: Is overnight parking allowed?**
  A: No, overnight parking is not permitted. Vehicles left overnight may be towed at the owner's expense.
- **Q: Are there discounts for parking?**
  A: Occasionally, annual pass holders or special promotions may offer reduced parking rates. Check the park's official website or inquire with guest services for current offers.

Parking at Universal Studios Hollywood doesn't have to be a headache. By choosing the right option for your needs and following these tips, you'll start your adventure off on the right foot.

Public Transportation and Shuttle Services to Universal Studios Hollywood

Getting to Universal Studios Hollywood via public transportation is not only eco-friendly but also cost-effective, especially for those looking to save money on parking and gas. Here's a comprehensive guide to navigating public transit options and shuttle services, complete with estimated costs to help you budget your trip effectively.

Public Transportation Options
1. Metro Red Line
The **Metro Red Line** subway is the most convenient and direct public transit option to Universal Studios Hollywood.

- **Route:**
    - Take the Metro Red Line and exit at **Universal City/Studio City Station**.
    - From there, board the **Universal Studios Hollywood Shuttle** for a quick ride to the park entrance (free of charge).
- **Cost:**
    - **Metro Base Fare:** $1.75 per ride.
    - **Day Pass:** $7 for unlimited rides on all Metro buses and trains.
    - Children under 5 ride free with a paying adult (limit of two children per adult).
- **Payment Options:**
    - Purchase a **TAP Card** ($2) from any Metro station or through the TAP app. Load your fare or passes onto the card.
- **Travel Time:**
    - From Downtown Los Angeles: ~15-20 minutes to Universal City Station.
    - From Hollywood: ~5-10 minutes.

2. Metro Bus Services

Metro buses also connect various parts of Los Angeles to Universal Studios Hollywood.

- **Key Bus Lines:**
  - **Metro Line 240:** Serves the San Fernando Valley and stops near Universal City.
  - **Metro Line 750 (Rapid Bus):** Offers faster service along Ventura Boulevard.
- **Cost:**
  - Same as the Metro Red Line: $1.75 per ride or $7 for a day pass.
- **Tips:**
  - Plan your route using the **Metro Trip Planner** on the official website or app.
  - Some buses may require a short walk to the shuttle station.

3. Regional Train Services

For those traveling from areas outside of Los Angeles, regional train services like **Metrolink** and **Amtrak** can connect to the Metro Red Line at Union Station.

- **Route:**
  - Take a Metrolink or Amtrak train to **Union Station**.
  - Transfer to the Metro Red Line heading toward **North Hollywood**.
  - Exit at **Universal City Station** and board the shuttle.
- **Cost:**
  - **Metrolink Fares:** Vary by distance, starting at $10 for a round trip within nearby counties.
  - **Amtrak Fares:** Start at ~$15 one-way for short distances, depending on your origin.

- **Travel Time:**
  - o Varies by origin. From Anaheim (Disneyland area), expect ~1-1.5 hours to Union Station by train.

4. FlyAway Bus Service

For visitors arriving at **Los Angeles International Airport (LAX)**, the FlyAway Bus is a convenient way to connect to the Metro system.
- **Route:**
  - o Board the FlyAway Bus from LAX to **Union Station**.
  - o Transfer to the Metro Red Line heading toward Universal City.
- **Cost:**
  - o **FlyAway Bus Fare:** $9.75 one way (per adult).
  - o Children under 5 ride free (limit of two per paying adult).
- **Travel Time:**
  - o ~30-50 minutes from LAX to Union Station, depending on traffic.

Universal Studios Hollywood Shuttle Service

Once you arrive at the **Universal City/Studio City Station**, the **Universal Studios Shuttle** provides complimentary transportation to the park entrance.
- **Cost:**
  - o Free for all visitors.
- **Frequency:**
  - o Shuttles run every 10-15 minutes during park hours.
- **Travel Time:**
  - o Less than 5 minutes from the station to the park.
- **Accessibility:**
  - o The shuttles are wheelchair accessible.

Sample Budget for Public Transportation

Origin	Transit Option	Cost (Round Trip)	Notes
Downtown Los Angeles	Metro Red Line	$3.50	Add $2 for a TAP card if you don't have one.
Hollywood	Metro Red Line	$3.50	Quickest and most affordable option.
Santa Monica	Metro Bus + Red Line	$7.00	Includes transfer between bus and subway.
Anaheim (Disneyland area)	Amtrak + Metro Red Line	~$40	Price varies depending on Amtrak tickets.
Los Angeles International (LAX)	FlyAway Bus + Metro Red Line	$27.50	Includes FlyAway Bus and Metro day pass.
Burbank	Metro Bus or Metrolink + Red Line	~$5-$10	Depending on your chosen route.

Money-Saving Tips

1. **Use a TAP Card:**
   Load a day pass if you plan on taking multiple trips throughout the day—it's more cost-effective than paying per ride.

2. **Travel During Off-Peak Hours:**
   Metro services are less crowded and often faster during non-commute hours (10 AM - 3 PM and after 7 PM).

3. **Group Discounts:**
   Check for group fare discounts if traveling with family or friends.
4. **Stay Near the Metro Red Line:**
   If you're staying overnight, book accommodations close to a Metro Red Line station to save time and money on transportation.
5. **Download the Metro App:**
   Use the app to track train and bus schedules, plan routes, and reload your TAP Card on the go.

Final Tips

- **Plan Ahead:** Research your transit options and schedules in advance to avoid delays.
- **Leave Early:** Arrive at least 30-60 minutes before the park opens to maximize your day.
- **Carry Essentials:** Keep your TAP Card, phone, and a small amount of cash for emergencies.
- **Be Patient:** Public transportation may take longer than driving, but it's stress-free and allows you to avoid parking fees.

With these public transportation options and shuttle services, getting to Universal Studios Hollywood can be both affordable and convenient, leaving you more time and money to enjoy your day at the park!

CHAPTER 3

Tickets and Packages

Types of Tickets – General Admission, Express, and VIP

Universal Studios Hollywood offers a range of ticket options to suit every guest's preferences, schedule, and budget. From the standard General Admission to skip-the-line privileges with the Express Pass, and even exclusive behind-the-scenes experiences with the VIP Pass, there's a ticket for every type of visitor. Let's dive into the details to help you choose the best option for your trip.

1. General Admission Tickets
General Admission tickets provide standard entry to the park, granting access to all attractions, shows, and rides for the day.

Cost
- **Pricing:** $109-$149 per person (varies by date, season, and demand).
- **Children (under 48"):** Typically $5-$10 less than adult tickets.
- **Toddlers (2 and under):** Free.

Best For
- First-time visitors on a budget.
- Guests who don't mind waiting in line during peak hours.
- Those visiting during non-peak seasons (e.g., weekdays or off-peak months like January and February).

What's Included
- Access to all rides, attractions, and entertainment shows.

- Entry to themed lands, including **The Wizarding World of Harry Potter** and **Super Nintendo World**.

Pros

- Most affordable ticket option.
- Great for visitors with flexible schedules or those planning to spend the entire day exploring the park.

Cons

- Long wait times for popular attractions during weekends and holidays.
- No re-entry privileges (unless specified).

2. Universal Express Tickets

Overview

The Universal Express ticket is the park's most popular upgrade, allowing you to skip the regular lines for rides, shows, and attractions once per experience.

Cost

- **Pricing:** $189-$279 per person (varies by date, season, and demand).
- **Children (under 48"):** Same price as adults.

Best For

- Visitors with limited time who want to experience as much as possible.
- Families with kids who might not tolerate long waits.
- Guests visiting during peak seasons (e.g., summer, holidays, or special events).

What's Included

- All benefits of General Admission.
- One-time express access to each ride, attraction, and seated show.

Pros

- Dramatically reduced wait times (often cutting lines by 75% or more).

- Allows for a more relaxed pace while still enjoying the park's highlights.

Cons
- Higher cost than General Admission.
- Express access is limited to one use per attraction; additional visits to the same attraction require waiting in the regular line.

Insider Tip:
- The Express ticket often sells out, especially during peak seasons. Book online and in advance to secure your spot.

3. VIP Experience Tickets

Overview

The VIP Experience offers the ultimate way to visit Universal Studios Hollywood, combining front-of-line access with an exclusive guided tour and behind-the-scenes access.

Cost
- **Pricing:** $369-$449 per person (varies by date and demand).
- **Children (under 48"):** Same price as adults.

Best For
- Hardcore Universal Studios fans.
- Guests celebrating a special occasion.
- Movie buffs who want an insider's look at Universal's film and TV production.

What's Included
- All benefits of General Admission and Express Pass.
- Unlimited express access to rides, attractions, and shows.
- A guided tour of the **Universal Studios Backlot**, including areas not accessible to the general public.
- Exclusive access to sound stages, props, and filming locations.
- A gourmet lunch in the **VIP Dining Lounge**.
- Complimentary valet parking.

Pros
- Skip all lines (unlimited express access).

- Enjoy an exclusive, behind-the-scenes look at Hollywood's movie-making magic.
- Premium dining and valet parking make the experience seamless.

Cons
- The most expensive ticket option.
- Requires advance booking, as space is limited.

Insider Tip:
- If you're traveling as a group, book together to ensure everyone is included in the same VIP tour group.

How to Choose the Right Ticket

Ticket Type	Best For	Budget Range	Key Perks
General Admission	Budget-conscious visitors or those with flexible schedules.	$109-$149	Access to all attractions and shows.
Universal Express	Time-savvy visitors or those visiting during peak seasons.	$189-$279	Skip the lines once per ride and show.
VIP Experience	Movie enthusiasts or those celebrating special occasions.	$369-$449	Behind-the-scenes tour, gourmet dining, unlimited express.

Money-Saving Tips for Tickets

1. **Buy Online:**
   Purchase tickets directly from the Universal Studios Hollywood website to save on gate prices and guarantee availability.
2. **Check for Promotions:**
   Look out for seasonal discounts, combo packages, or special deals through third-party vendors like Costco or AAA.

3. **Go Off-Peak:**
   Ticket prices are often lower on weekdays and during the off-season.
4. **Annual Pass:**
   If you're planning to visit more than once, consider an **Annual Pass,**

which offers unlimited access on select dates and additional perks like discounts on dining, shopping, and parking. Prices for annual passes start at $219 and can be a cost-effective option for frequent visitors.

Special Packages and Bundles
1. Combo Tickets

Combine your visit to Universal Studios Hollywood with other attractions in Los Angeles, such as Disneyland, Knott's Berry Farm, or the Warner Bros. Studio Tour.

- **Pricing:** Varies depending on the attractions included, typically starting at $200-$300 for two or more parks.
- **Best For:** Visitors planning a multi-day vacation and wanting to experience more of Southern California's theme parks.

2. Hotel + Ticket Packages

Universal Studios partners with nearby hotels to offer discounted rates when booking your park tickets and accommodations together.

- **Pricing:** Packages vary, starting at around $300 per night (including hotel stay and park tickets).
- **Best For:** Out-of-town visitors looking for convenience and savings on lodging and tickets.

3. Seasonal Events Packages

Universal Studios Hollywood frequently hosts special events like **Halloween Horror Nights** and **Grinchmas**, which may include unique ticket packages with early entry, exclusive experiences, or themed dining options.

- **Pricing:** Event ticket prices vary, starting at $80 for Halloween Horror Nights and higher for add-ons like express access.
- **Best For:** Fans of seasonal festivities and limited-time park experiences.

Final Tips
- **Plan Ahead:** Popular ticket types, especially Express and VIP, sell out quickly during peak times, so book as early as possible.
- **Travel with a Group:** Group discounts may be available for parties of 10 or more—contact the park for details.
- **Download the App:** Use the Universal Studios Hollywood app to keep track of wait times, show schedules, and your ticket information.

By understanding the different ticket options and choosing the one that fits your budget and priorities, you'll ensure a seamless and unforgettable visit to Universal Studios Hollywood!

Annual Passes: Benefits and Cost Analysis

For frequent visitors or those planning multiple trips to Universal Studios Hollywood, an annual pass can be an excellent investment. Annual passes offer flexibility, discounts, and access to special perks that make every visit even more enjoyable. Here's a detailed breakdown of the types of annual passes, their benefits, costs, and how to decide if it's the right choice for you.

Types of Annual Passes

Pass Type	Cost (2025 Pricing)	Key Features
California Neighbor Pass	$219/year	Affordable option for SoCal residents; limited access to specific weekdays and non-peak seasons.
Silver Pass	$299/year	Access on most weekdays and some weekends; black-out dates apply during peak seasons.
Gold Pass	$459/year	Access on most days of the year, including some peak dates; free parking and discounts included.
Platinum Pass	$759/year	Unlimited access with no black-out dates; priority perks like Express after 3 PM and VIP parking.

Detailed Benefits of Each Pass
1. California Neighbor Pass
- **Target Audience:** Southern California residents looking for an affordable option to visit on non-peak days.
- **Access:** 170+ select days annually, excluding weekends and peak seasons.
- **Perks:**

- o Discounts on food and merchandise (10%).
- o Discounts on additional tickets for friends and family.
- **Drawbacks:**
  - o Significant black-out dates, including holidays and summer weekends.

2. Silver Pass

- **Target Audience:** Occasional visitors who prefer visiting on weekdays with occasional weekend access.
- **Access:** 250+ days annually, with some black-out dates during peak times.
- **Perks:**
  - o Food and merchandise discounts (10%).
  - o Early park entry on select days.
- **Drawbacks:**
  - o No free parking.
  - o Restricted during major holidays and high-traffic weekends.

3. Gold Pass

- **Target Audience:** Frequent visitors who want more flexibility and added perks.
- **Access:** ~325 days annually, including select peak dates.
- **Perks:**
  - o Free general parking (saves $30 per visit).
  - o Food and merchandise discounts (15%).
  - o Early park entry on select days.
  - o Discounts on Halloween Horror Nights tickets.
- **Drawbacks:**
  - o A handful of black-out dates during the busiest times of the year.

4. Platinum Pass

- **Target Audience:** Die-hard fans and families looking for the ultimate experience with unlimited access and premium perks.
- **Access:** 365 days annually with no black-out dates.
- **Perks:**
    o Free valet or preferred parking (saves $50 per visit).
    o Unlimited Express Pass after 3 PM (saves hours in line).
    o Food and merchandise discounts (20%).
    o Exclusive invitations to special events and previews.
    o Discounts on Halloween Horror Nights tickets.
- **Drawbacks:**
    o Higher upfront cost.

Cost Analysis: Is an Annual Pass Worth It?
General Admission vs. Annual Pass

- A single-day General Admission ticket ranges from $109-$149.
- If you plan to visit the park at least **3-5 times a year**, even the most basic annual pass (California Neighbor Pass) becomes cost-effective.

Perks vs. Price

- **Parking Savings:**
    o General parking costs $30 per visit, while valet or preferred parking is $50.
    o A Gold or Platinum Pass includes free parking, making it a great value for frequent drivers.
- **Express Pass Value:**
    o Unlimited Express Passes can cost $189-$279 for a single day.
    o The Platinum Pass includes **Unlimited Express access after 3 PM**, which quickly offsets its higher cost.

- **Discounts on Food & Merchandise:**
  - Average theme park meals cost ~$15-$20.
  - With a 10%-20% discount, savings can add up over multiple visits.

Example Cost Breakdown:

Scenario	Number of Visits Per Year	Ticket/Pass Cost	Parking Savings	Express Access Savings	Food Savings	Total Value
General Admission (5 visits)	5	$545-$745	$150	N/A	N/A	$695-$895
Silver Pass	5	$299	$0	N/A	~$30	~$329
Gold Pass (with parking)	5	$459	$150	N/A	~$40	~$649
Platinum Pass (with Express)	5	$759	$250	~$750 (Express after 3 PM)	~$50	~$1,809

When to Choose an Annual Pass

An annual pass makes sense if:

- You plan to visit at least 3-4 times a year.
- You want perks like free parking, food discounts, or Express access.
- You're a Southern California resident looking for convenient, frequent visits.
- You want the flexibility of visiting on multiple dates without buying tickets each time.

Money-Saving Tips for Annual Passholders
1. **Plan Visits on Non-Black-Out Dates:** Check the calendar to maximize your access based on your pass type.
2. **Take Advantage of Discounts:** Use food, merchandise, and ticket discounts to save even more on each visit.
3. **Upgrade Your Pass:** If you find yourself visiting more often, you can upgrade to a higher-tier pass by paying the difference.
4. **Buy During Promotions:** Universal Studios occasionally offers discounts or added perks for annual pass purchases, especially during off-peak times.

Annual passes are a great way to enjoy Universal Studios Hollywood year-round while saving money and unlocking exclusive perks. For casual visitors, the California Neighbor or Silver Pass provides affordable access. For die-hard fans, the Gold or Platinum Pass offers premium perks that enhance every visit. Evaluate your schedule, budget, and priorities to determine which pass suits you best!

Seasonal Promotions and Discounts

Universal Studios Hollywood frequently offers seasonal promotions and discounts to make your visit more affordable. These deals often coincide with holidays, special events, or off-peak seasons, making them a great opportunity to save while enjoying unique park experiences. Let's explore the details to help you take full advantage of these offers.

1. Types of Seasonal Promotions

a. Off-Peak Discounts

- **When:** Typically offered during slower periods, such as weekdays in January, February, and September.
- **Details:** Tickets can be up to 20-30% cheaper during off-peak times compared to peak dates like weekends or holidays.
- **Example:** General Admission tickets may drop to $109 during off-peak times versus $149 on peak dates.

b. Holiday and Event Packages

- **When:** Available during major holidays (e.g., Halloween, Christmas, and Spring Break) and special events like **Halloween Horror Nights** or **Grinchmas**.
- **Details:** Packages may include early park entry, meal vouchers, or express access to specific event attractions.
- **Example:** Halloween Horror Nights often has discounted bundles, including admission and skip-the-line passes for select haunted houses.

c. Black Friday and Cyber Monday Deals

- **When:** Annually in late November.
- **Details:** Universal Studios Hollywood often offers deep discounts on tickets and annual passes for a limited time.
- **Example:** In previous years, visitors saved up to 40% on multi-day tickets or received bonus perks like free parking or food vouchers with annual passes.

d. Multi-Park Bundles

- **When:** Year-round, but often promoted during summer or holiday travel seasons.
- **Details:** Discounted rates for visiting Universal Studios Hollywood along with other Southern California attractions, such as Disneyland, Knott's Berry Farm, or SeaWorld.
- **Example:** A combo ticket might save you $50-$100 compared to purchasing tickets separately.

e. Group Discounts

- **When:** Year-round, but especially popular during school vacation periods or corporate retreats.
- **Details:** Groups of 10 or more can receive discounted rates on General Admission tickets.
- **Example:** Discounts typically range from 10-15% off the standard ticket price.

2. Membership and Affiliate Discounts

a. AAA Members

- **Details:** AAA members often receive discounted tickets when purchased in advance through AAA Travel offices.
- **Savings:** ~$5-$10 off General Admission or special rates for Express Passes.

b. Costco and Other Retailers

- **Details:** Costco and select retailers sometimes sell Universal Studios Hollywood tickets at reduced prices, often bundled with meal or parking vouchers.
- **Example:** A General Admission ticket bundled with a $20 dining credit may cost the same as a regular ticket.

c. Military Discounts

- **Details:** Active-duty and retired military personnel can access discounted tickets through authorized military ticket offices.
- **Savings:** ~10-15% off standard ticket prices.

3. How to Stay Updated on Promotions

- **Subscribe to Newsletters:** Sign up for Universal Studios Hollywood's email list to receive the latest deals and discounts directly to your inbox.
- **Follow Social Media:** Promotions are often announced on Universal's official social media accounts.
- **Third-Party Travel Sites:** Websites like Undercover Tourist or Get Away Today often feature exclusive deals and bundles.

Booking Online vs. At the Gate

Universal Studios Hollywood strongly encourages online bookings, and for good reason—there are significant advantages to purchasing tickets in advance through their website or authorized third-party vendors. Here's a detailed comparison:

1. Booking Online
Advantages:

- **Discounted Prices:** Online prices are almost always lower than gate prices.
  - **Example:** A General Admission ticket purchased online might cost $109, while the same ticket at the gate is $129.
- **Guaranteed Entry:** The park can sell out on busy days, but online tickets ensure you won't be turned away.
- **Special Offers:** Seasonal discounts, multi-day packages, and Express Passes are often available only online.
- **Flexibility:** Choose date-specific tickets to save even more, or opt for flexible-date tickets if your schedule is uncertain.
- **Skip the Lines:** Online tickets can be scanned directly from your smartphone, saving time at entry.

How to Book:

- Visit the official **Universal Studios Hollywood website** or trusted third-party sellers like **Undercover Tourist** or **Get Away Today**.
- Use the Universal Studios app to track ticket promotions and wait times for attractions.

Pro Tip: Check for promo codes before completing your purchase. Websites like RetailMeNot sometimes have additional discounts for Universal tickets.

2. Booking at the Gate

Advantages:

- **Last-Minute Flexibility:** Perfect for spontaneous visits if you're unsure of your schedule.
- **Immediate Access:** No need to print or download tickets in advance.

Disadvantages:

- **Higher Prices:** Gate prices are consistently more expensive than online rates, sometimes by $20 or more per ticket.
- **Risk of Sell-Out:** Tickets, especially for special events like Halloween Horror Nights, may sell out by the time you arrive.
- **Fewer Options:** Limited availability of upgrades like Express Passes or VIP Packages compared to booking online.

Pro Tip: If you must buy tickets at the gate, arrive early to avoid long lines and maximize your park time.

Cost Comparison: Online vs. Gate

Ticket Type	Online Price	Gate Price	Savings
General Admission	$109-$129	$129-$149	~$20
Express Pass	$189-$279	$209-$299	~$30-$40
VIP Experience	$369-$449	$399-$479	~$30

When to Book Online vs. At the Gate

Scenario	Best Option
Planning in advance	Book online for discounts and guaranteed entry.
Visiting on a peak day or holiday	Book online to avoid sell-outs.
Spontaneous visit on a non-peak day	Gate purchase works but costs more.
Looking for bundled packages or upgrades	Book online for better options.

Whether you're a budget-conscious traveler or a luxury-seeking visitor, keeping an eye on seasonal promotions and booking online are key to saving money and maximizing your Universal Studios Hollywood experience. By planning ahead, taking advantage of discounts, and avoiding last-minute gate purchases, you can make your trip smooth, stress-free, and affordable.

CHAPTER 4

Navigating the Park: Park Layout - Upper Lot and Lower Lot

Universal Studios Hollywood is uniquely designed, with its attractions and amenities spread across two distinct levels: the **Upper Lot** and the **Lower Lot**, connected by a series of massive escalators known as the **Starway**. Each section offers a unique mix of entertainment, rides, dining, and shopping, so understanding the layout is crucial to planning your day efficiently. Here's a vivid, detailed guide to help you navigate the park like a pro.

Upper Lot: The Heart of the Park

The **Upper Lot** is the main entry point to Universal Studios Hollywood and is packed with some of the park's most iconic attractions, family-friendly experiences, and vibrant themed areas. It's where the magic begins!

Main Highlights
1. **The Wizarding World of Harry Potter**
    o Step into the magical village of **Hogsmeade**, complete with snow-topped roofs and cobblestone streets.
    o **Must-See Attractions:**
        ▪ *Harry Potter and the Forbidden Journey*: An immersive, 4D ride through Hogwarts Castle.
        ▪ *Flight of the Hippogriff*: A family-friendly roller coaster.
    o **Don't Miss:** Sip on a frothy Butterbeer or pick up a wand at Ollivanders for an interactive park experience.
2. **Springfield: Home of The Simpsons**

- o Enter the world of America's favorite animated family in this colorful, bustling area.
- o **Must-See Attractions:**
    - ▪ *The Simpsons Ride*: A hilarious motion simulator journey through Krustyland.
- o **Dining Options:**
    - ▪ Enjoy a Krusty Burger, a Lard Lad Donut, or a Duff Beer.

3. **Despicable Me Minion Mayhem**
   - o A 3D motion simulator ride that takes you into the wild and wacky world of the Minions.
   - o **For Families:** The adjacent **Super Silly Fun Land** is a playful, water-themed playground for kids.

4. **DreamWorks Theatre Featuring Kung Fu Panda**
   - o A multi-sensory 4D adventure with Po and his friends, showcasing stunning visuals and effects.

5. **Studio Tour Entrance**
   - o The world-famous **Studio Tour** departs from the Upper Lot, offering a behind-the-scenes look at real movie sets and special effects. Highlights include:
       - ▪ *King Kong 360 3D*
       - ▪ *Fast & Furious - Supercharged*
       - ▪ Classic backlot sets like the Bates Motel and the plane crash scene from *War of the Worlds*.

Dining and Shopping
- • **Dining:**
    - o *Three Broomsticks*: Enjoy British-inspired meals like fish and chips or shepherd's pie.
    - o *Mel's Diner*: A retro-themed eatery serving burgers and shakes.
- • **Shopping:**

- o *Universal Studios Store*: A one-stop shop for park merchandise.
- o *Honeydukes*: A sweet-tooth paradise featuring chocolate frogs and Bertie Bott's Every Flavour Beans.

Lower Lot: Thrills and Blockbusters

The **Lower Lot** is the smaller of the two levels but is packed with high-intensity attractions based on blockbuster movies. Prepare for an adrenaline rush as you descend the **Starway**, offering stunning views of the San Fernando Valley.

Main Highlights

1. **Jurassic World – The Ride**
   - o A thrilling water adventure through a world where dinosaurs roam freely.
   - o **Don't Miss:** The jaw-dropping finale featuring the colossal **Indominus Rex** battling the **T-Rex**.
   - o **Pro Tip:** Be prepared to get wet—ponchos are available for purchase.

2. **Transformers: The Ride-3D**
   - o A cutting-edge 3D experience that combines motion simulation and live-action effects.
   - o **Highlight:** Join Optimus Prime and Bumblebee in an epic battle against the Decepticons.

3. **Revenge of the Mummy – The Ride**
   - o A high-speed indoor roller coaster with dark, spooky twists and turns.
   - o **For Thrill-Seekers:** This ride is one of the most intense in the park, featuring sudden launches and backward motion.

4. **Raptor Encounter and Dino Play**
   - o Meet life-like dinosaurs, including Blue, the velociraptor, in an interactive photo-op experience.
   - o Kids can explore the **Dino Play** area for some prehistoric fun.

Dining and Shopping

- **Dining:**
    - *Jurassic Café*: Savor island-inspired dishes like roasted chicken and Costa Rican-themed plates.
    - *Panda Express*: A quick-service option for Asian-inspired meals.
- **Shopping:**
    - *Transformers Supply Vault*: Gear up with Transformers-themed merchandise.
    - *Jurassic Outfitters*: Find dinosaur-themed souvenirs, apparel, and toys.

The Starway: Connecting Upper and Lower Lots

The **Starway** is a series of four massive outdoor escalators that transport guests between the Upper and Lower Lots.

Key Features:

- **Scenic Views:** The Starway offers panoramic views of the San Fernando Valley—great for photos!
- **Time Estimate:** It takes about 5-7 minutes to travel from one lot to the other.
- **Rest Areas:** Benches are available along the way if you need a breather.

Pro Tips:

- Plan your day to minimize trips between the Upper and Lower Lots, as the journey can be time-consuming.
- Visit the Lower Lot attractions early or late in the day to avoid long lines during peak hours.

Tips for Navigating the Park

1. **Start Early:** Arrive at the park as soon as it opens and head straight to popular attractions like **Jurassic World** or **The Wizarding World of Harry Potter**.

2. **Use the Universal Studios App:** The app provides a real-time park map, wait times, and show schedules, helping you plan your route efficiently.
3. **Plan for Peak Times:** The park gets busier around noon, so schedule rides with long wait times for early morning or evening.
4. **Know Your Priorities:** Decide which attractions are must-dos and visit those first.
5. **Dining Reservations:** For popular dining spots like *Three Broomsticks*, make reservations or plan to eat during off-peak hours.

Navigating Universal Studios Hollywood is a breeze when you understand its two-tier layout. The **Upper Lot** offers a blend of magical, family-friendly experiences and classic attractions, while the **Lower Lot** packs a punch with thrilling rides and blockbuster adventures. By planning your route, using the Starway strategically, and prioritizing your favorite attractions, you'll make the most of your day in this cinematic wonderland.

Understanding Wait Times and Crowd Flow: The Universal Studios App as Your Digital Companion

When visiting Universal Studios Hollywood, managing your time effectively is crucial to enjoying as many attractions as possible. The Universal Studios App is an essential tool that provides real-time updates on wait times, show schedules, and crowd patterns, helping you navigate the park efficiently. This step-by-step guide will show you how to use the app to optimize your visit.

Step 1: Downloading and Setting Up the App
1. **Locate the App:**
    o Search for **"Universal Studios Hollywood"** in the App Store (iOS) or Google Play Store (Android).
    o Ensure the app is the official one by Universal Parks & Resorts.
2. **Download and Install:**
    o Tap "Download" or "Install" and wait for the app to install on your device.
3. **Create an Account (Optional):**
    o Open the app and create an account for personalized features like saving favorites, setting alerts, and managing tickets.
    o Use the same email associated with your tickets to sync them directly to the app.
4. **Allow Permissions:**
    o Enable location services for real-time updates on wait times and proximity-based notifications.

Step 2: Navigating the Home Screen

Once the app is set up, you'll see a user-friendly interface with several key sections:

1. **Park Map:**
   o An interactive map that shows ride locations, restaurants, restrooms, and more.
   o Use the zoom feature to see details or tap icons for specific information.

2. **Wait Times:**
   o A real-time list of current wait times for each attraction.
   o Sorted by location (Upper Lot and Lower Lot) or popularity.

3. **Showtimes:**
   o A schedule for live shows and entertainment like the **WaterWorld Stunt Show** or the **Special Effects Show**.

4. **Dining and Shopping:**
   o A list of restaurants and shops, including their menus and locations.

5. **Alerts and Notifications:**
   o Notifications for changes in wait times, special events, or ride closures.

Step 3: Using the App for Wait Times

1. **Locate Wait Times:**
   o Tap the "Wait Times" section on the home screen or select an attraction on the map to see its current wait time.

2. **Analyze Patterns:**
   o Pay attention to fluctuating wait times. Popular attractions like *Jurassic World* and *Harry Potter and*

the Forbidden Journey may have shorter waits early in the morning or late in the evening.

3. **Set Alerts:**
   - For your favorite rides, set alerts to notify you when the wait time drops below a certain threshold.

4. **Pro Tip:**
   - Combine short wait times with nearby attractions to maximize efficiency. For example, visit *The Simpsons Ride* after checking the wait for *Despicable Me Minion Mayhem.*

Step 4: Planning Around Crowd Flow

1. **Understand Crowd Flow Patterns:**
   - Mornings: Crowds are lightest during the first 1-2 hours after park opening. Head to high-demand attractions first.
   - Midday: Lines tend to peak around noon. Use this time for shows, dining, or exploring less busy areas.
   - Evening: Wait times typically decrease for major attractions an hour before the park closes.

2. **Check Peak Times for Rides:**
   - The app shows peak wait times for each ride throughout the day. Use this data to plan breaks or visit less crowded areas.

3. **Utilize the Starway Timing:**
   - If transitioning between the **Upper Lot** and **Lower Lot**, plan around mid-afternoon crowds. The app can indicate if certain areas are more crowded.

Step 5: Maximizing the App's Features
1. **Interactive Map for Navigation:**
   - Tap the map icon to plot your route based on your current location. The app provides step-by-step directions to rides, dining, and amenities.
2. **Dining Reservations:**
   - Use the app to reserve tables at popular eateries like *Three Broomsticks* or *Jurassic Café*.
   - View restaurant menus to decide on meals ahead of time.
3. **Show Notifications:**
   - Set reminders for live shows, character meet-and-greets, or special events.
4. **Mobile Ticketing:**
   - Link your tickets in the app for quick scanning at the gate or when upgrading to Express or VIP passes.
5. **Express Pass Tracking:**
   - If you purchase an Express Pass, the app highlights express queue entrances, helping you skip regular lines.

Step 6: Dealing with Ride Closures or Delays
1. **Real-Time Updates:**
   - The app notifies you immediately if a ride is temporarily closed due to maintenance or weather conditions.
2. **Alternate Plans:**
   - Use the app to identify nearby attractions or dining options to fill unexpected gaps in your schedule.
3. **Virtual Line for Select Attractions:**
   - Some rides may offer a virtual line feature through the app, allowing you to reserve a spot and return later.

Pro Tips for Using the Universal Studios App
1. **Battery Management:**
    o The app can drain your phone's battery quickly. Bring a portable charger or rent a charging locker at the park.
2. **Wi-Fi Connectivity:**
    o Universal Studios Hollywood offers free Wi-Fi throughout the park. Connect to it for faster app performance and to save data.
3. **Family and Group Features:**
    o If you're visiting with a group, share your plans and wait time updates using the app.
4. **Refresh Regularly:**
    o Wait times can change rapidly. Refresh the app every 10-15 minutes to stay updated.

    o

The Universal Studios App is your ultimate digital companion for navigating the park. From tracking wait times to understanding crowd flow and planning dining, this tool streamlines your experience and ensures you spend less time waiting and more time enjoying the magic. By mastering the app's features, you'll make the most of your visit and create unforgettable memories.

CHAPTER 5

All Attractions and Rides at Universal Studios Hollywood

Upper Lot Attractions and Rides
1. **The Wizarding World of Harry Potter**
   - **Harry Potter and the Forbidden Journey**
   - **Flight of the Hippogriff**
   - **Ollivanders Wand Experience**
2. **Springfield: Home of The Simpsons**
   - **The Simpsons Ride**
   - **Krustyland** (Themed area)
   - **Fast Food Blvd** (Dining area)
3. **Despicable Me Minion Mayhem**
4. **DreamWorks Theatre Featuring Kung Fu Panda**
5. **Studio Tour** (Behind-the-scenes studio tram tour)
   - *King Kong 360 3D*
   - *Fast & Furious – Supercharged*
   - *War of the Worlds* (Plane crash set)
   - *The Jaws Set*
   - *The Bates Motel (Psycho)*
6. **The Walking Dead Attraction**
7. **WaterWorld** (Live action stunt show)

Lower Lot Attractions and Rides
   - **Jurassic World – The Ride**
   - **Transformers: The Ride-3D**
   - **Revenge of the Mummy – The Ride**
   - **Raptor Encounter** (Meet and greet with raptors)

- **Dino Play** (Interactive play area for kids)

Additional Attractions
- **Super Silly Fun Land** (Located near Despicable Me)
- **Studio Store** (Shops located throughout the park for various Universal-themed merchandise)

These attractions and rides offer a mix of family-friendly experiences, thrilling rides, and interactive shows, all catering to a wide range of visitors.

Upper Lot

The Wizarding World of Harry Potter & Despicable Me: Minion Mayhem

The **Upper Lot** at Universal Studios Hollywood is home to two of the most immersive and enchanting themed areas in the park. First, step into the magical world of **The Wizarding World of Harry Potter**, where you can experience Hogwarts Castle and the thrilling **Flight of the Hippogriff**. Then, unleash your inner child in **Despicable Me: Minion Mayhem**, where the mischievous Minions lead you into their chaotic and hilarious world. Let's dive into these areas in vivid detail.

The Wizarding World of Harry Potter
This enchanted land is a must-see for **Harry Potter** fans, transporting you right into the heart of **Hogsmeade**, the magical village from the books and films. The area is a masterpiece of theme park design, from the snow-capped rooftops of the shops to the towering spires of **Hogwarts Castle**—it's like stepping straight into the pages of the beloved wizarding world.

Must-See Attractions in The Wizarding World
1. **Harry Potter and the Forbidden Journey**
   o **Description:** This is a groundbreaking, motion-simulator ride that takes you through the iconic **Hogwarts Castle**. The ride seamlessly blends **4D technology** with live-action, offering a truly magical experience as you soar through the skies with Harry Potter, Hermione Granger, Ron Weasley, and other beloved characters.

- Highlights:
  - Fly above the Quidditch pitch.
  - Face terrifying creatures like **Dementors** and the **Acromantula** (giant spiders).
  - Get caught in a thrilling chase through the corridors of Hogwarts, where you'll feel like you're actually there.
- **Pro Tip:** This ride has some intense moments and may not be suitable for younger or sensitive guests. Riders must be at least 48 inches tall.

2. **Flight of the Hippogriff**
   - **Description:** A family-friendly roller coaster that's perfect for younger adventurers, this ride is a gentle journey on the back of a **Hippogriff**, a magical creature that's half eagle, half horse. The ride is set in the grounds of Hogwarts, passing by **Hagrid's Hut** and the **Hippogriff's nest**.
   - **Highlights:**
     - A smooth but exciting first drop, followed by several gentle twists and turns.
     - The chance to see Hagrid's hut and learn more about the creatures of the wizarding world.
   - **Pro Tip:** This is a great first coaster for younger kids or those new to thrill rides.

3. **Ollivanders Wand Shop Experience**
   - **Description:** While not a ride, this interactive experience is a must-do. Enter the famous **Ollivanders Wand Shop** for a magical **wand selection ceremony** where a lucky guest may be chosen to receive their wand in a scene reminiscent of the Harry Potter films.
   - **Highlights:**
     - See real wands from the films on display.

- Experience magic firsthand as objects come to life in the shop, offering a truly immersive and enchanting moment.
4. **Hogwarts Castle**
    o **Description:** The towering, snow-covered castle is the centerpiece of the land, offering more than just a place for the ride. Stroll through the grounds and visit key locations like the **Gryffindor Common Room** and the **Hogwarts Hallway**, with hidden details and magical surprises around every corner.
    o **Pro Tip:** Take time to explore the castle even if you're not riding the Forbidden Journey; it's a spectacle worth enjoying at a leisurely pace.

Dining & Shopping
- **Three Broomsticks**: The rustic, cozy pub offers hearty British fare such as fish and chips, shepherd's pie, and the famous **Butterbeer**—a sweet, frothy beverage that's a fan-favorite.
- **Honeydukes**: A whimsical candy shop where you can find magical treats like chocolate frogs, jelly beans (Bertie Bott's Every Flavor Beans), and pumpkin pasties.
- **Filch's Emporium of Confiscated Goods**: An official shop for all things Hogwarts, from robes to house scarves and collectible items.

Despicable Me: Minion Mayhem

Next, dive into the **Despicable Me Minion Mayhem**, a chaotic and hilarious 3D motion-simulator ride based on the beloved **Despicable Me** movies. This area is filled with mischief, fun, and Minions, making it an excellent choice for families and fans of the films.

Must-See Attractions in Despicable Me
1. **Despicable Me Minion Mayhem**
    o **Description:** This 3D motion-simulator ride takes you on a wild journey as you join Gru, the girls, and the

mischievous Minions. The ride is a perfect blend of humor and action, with moments of laughter, surprises, and some delightful mayhem.

- o **Highlights:**
  - Take part in **Gru's Minionization** process, where you become a Minion and experience the world from their point of view.
  - The motion-simulation effects are top-notch, making you feel like you're part of the action, whether it's soaring through the air or getting caught in the chaos.
  - Expect plenty of **Minion-style slapstick humor** and silly moments that will leave both kids and adults laughing.
- o **Pro Tip:** This ride has a gentle motion, but it does include 3D effects, so if you're sensitive to motion sickness, you might want to take precautions before riding.

2. **Super Silly Fun Land**
   - o **Description:** A colorful, water-themed play area located adjacent to the **Minion Mayhem** ride, **Super Silly Fun Land** is a perfect spot for families with younger children to burn off some energy. It features interactive water fountains, carnival-style games, and fun, Minion-themed activities.
   - o **Highlights:**
     - The **Minion Mayhem Balloon Ride** is a gentle ride for kids, offering a whimsical view of the land.
     - Splash zones where kids can cool off and play.
   - o **Pro Tip:** If you're visiting during warmer months, this is the perfect place for your little ones to cool down.

Dining & Shopping
- **Fried Chicken & Tots Stand**: Enjoy a quick meal of crispy chicken and tater tots, perfect for refueling after all the fun.
- **Super Silly Stuff**: A souvenir shop packed with Minion-themed merchandise, from plush toys to Minion-themed apparel, making it the ultimate destination for taking home a piece of the fun.

Tips for Enjoying These Attractions
- **Timing is Everything**: Arrive early to experience **Harry Potter and the Forbidden Journey** with shorter wait times, especially if you're visiting during peak hours.
- **Use the Universal Studios Hollywood App**: Keep an eye on real-time wait times for both the Wizarding World and Minion Mayhem rides.
- **Get Interactive**: Don't just rush through the attractions—take time to engage with the surroundings. For instance, try casting spells with the interactive wands around Hogsmeade or enjoy the humorous antics of the Minions during the ride.
- **Food Breaks**: If you're craving something sweet, **Butterbeer** and candy from **Honeydukes** are the perfect picks. For a quick bite, stop by the **Fried Chicken & Tots Stand** near **Minion Mayhem**.

The **Upper Lot** at Universal Studios Hollywood offers a dazzling combination of magical and comedic experiences, with **The Wizarding World of Harry Potter** bringing the enchantment of the Hogwarts universe to life and **Despicable Me: Minion Mayhem** delivering non-stop laughs and playful chaos. Whether you're a **Harry Potter** enthusiast or a fan of **Minions**, these areas promise an unforgettable and immersive experience for visitors of all ages.

Upper Lot: The Simpsons Ride & Secret Life of Pets: Off the Leash

Two of Universal Studios Hollywood's most exciting attractions reside in the **Upper Lot**—**The Simpsons Ride** and **Secret Life of Pets: Off the Leash**. Each brings its own brand of high-energy thrills, laughs, and heartwarming moments, making them must-do attractions for any visitor. Let's dive deep into each of these rides and experiences to help you make the most of your time at the park.

The Simpsons Ride

Step into the colorful and wacky world of **Springfield** with **The Simpsons Ride**, one of the most entertaining 3D motion simulator rides in the park. The ride brings the iconic characters from **The Simpsons** TV show to life, taking you on a hilarious, action-packed adventure filled with quirky antics, outrageous humor, and plenty of surprises.

Overview and Highlights

- **Storyline:**

  In **The Simpsons Ride**, you join Homer, Marge, Bart, Lisa, and Maggie as they visit **Krustyland**, a theme park created by the mischievous and bumbling **Krusty the Clown**. After a series of unexpected events (because, of course, it's Homer Simpson), you're launched into a chaotic, fun-filled experience that includes a series of wacky mishaps, surreal attractions, and crazy stunts.

- **Ride Experience:**

  - The ride is a **motion simulator** that uses **3D technology** to make you feel as though you're truly part of the action. You'll be thrust through Krustyland's wild and unpredictable attractions, including a stomach-churning roller coaster, all while being bombarded with the show's iconic humor.

- o The 3D effects are top-notch, with surprising drops, sudden movements, and a fully immersive experience that feels just like you're on an animated adventure with **Bart**, **Homer**, **Marge**, and the rest of the gang.
- o **Highlights of the Ride:**
  - A **speeding rollercoaster** through Krustyland, full of twists, loops, and wild motions.
  - An **escape from the clutches of Sideshow Bob**, the show's lovable antagonist.
  - Classic **Simpsons humor**—expect rapid-fire jokes and references to the show's long-running gags.
  - A **dramatic finale**, complete with Krusty's schemes spiraling out of control.

Pro Tips

- **For Families:** This ride has moderate thrills and is suitable for older children and adults. Kids must be at least **40 inches tall** to ride.
- **Brace Yourself:** If you're prone to motion sickness, prepare for a fast-paced, dizzying experience. Grab some **motion sickness tablets** or take a quick break afterward.
- **Maximize Fun:** To avoid long wait times, try riding early in the morning or later in the evening when crowds have thinned out.

Dining & Shopping Nearby

- **Krusty Burger:** Grab a classic fast-food burger at **Krusty's**, with a variety of options that mimic the silly, over-the-top nature of **Springfield**.
- **Lard Lad Donuts:** Don't miss out on the oversized donuts, a quirky, sweet treat that's a Springfield classic.
- **The Simpsons Store:** Shop for **Simpsons**-themed merch, from T-shirts and mugs to the iconic **Lard Lad** figurines and **Krusty the Clown** memorabilia.

Secret Life of Pets: Off the Leash

Inspired by the popular animated films, **Secret Life of Pets: Off the Leash** invites guests into a world where pets are secretly living full lives when their owners aren't around. This interactive, family-friendly dark ride offers heartwarming moments, thrills, and plenty of adorable animals, bringing the beloved movie characters to life in a new and exciting way.

Overview and Highlights

- **Storyline:**

  Join your pet pals as you take a journey through the world of **Max**, **Duke**, and other adorable animals featured in the **Secret Life of Pets** films. The ride immerses you in the bustling streets of New York City, where you'll experience life as a pet in an oversized world, encountering all kinds of funny, quirky, and unexpected situations.

- **Ride Experience:**

  - The attraction is a **trackless ride**, allowing for a more dynamic and spontaneous journey, with each ride offering unique experiences. As you board, you get to join Max and his furry friends in the heart of the city.

  - The ride features **advanced technology**, combining **3D projections**, **physical sets**, and **animatronics** to bring the pet world to life.

  - **Highlights of the Ride:**

    - Get up close to Max, Duke, and the other characters as you journey through a beautifully detailed New York City, full of vibrant neighborhoods and playful scenes.

    - Experience interactive moments where your choices can influence the ride's outcome, letting you feel even more involved.

    - Watch as pets and humans interact in whimsical, larger-than-life environments, from city rooftops to parks filled with mischievous animals.

Pro Tips

- **Family Fun:** This ride is a perfect choice for families, including young children, as it's filled with humor and warmth but lacks the intense thrills of other rides in the park.
- **Experience the Detail:** Take a moment to appreciate the attention to detail in the pet world, from the city's busy streets to the quirky animal antics.
- **Ride Photos:** This is one of the few attractions where your photo can be captured during the ride, so be ready for some fun moments.

Dining & Shopping Nearby

- **Pets' Playground:** After enjoying the ride, take a moment to explore the pet-themed **interactive play area**, perfect for kids to run off some energy.
- **Pet-Themed Merchandise:** Stop by the gift shop for cute pet-related merchandise, from plush toys to apparel inspired by the lovable characters from the **Secret Life of Pets** franchise.

Tips for Enjoying Both Rides

1. **Timing Your Visit:**
   - Since both **The Simpsons Ride** and **Secret Life of Pets: Off the Leash** are extremely popular, try to experience them early in the day or closer to park closing to minimize wait times.
   - Use the **Universal Studios Hollywood app** for real-time updates on ride wait times and show schedules to help you plan efficiently.
2. **For Young Kids:**
   - **Secret Life of Pets: Off the Leash** is perfect for younger kids due to its less-intense, charming nature.

The Simpsons Ride, while fun, is best suited for older kids and adults due to its motion simulation.

- o   Keep an eye out for photo ops with **Simpsons characters** and the adorable **pets** from the movie!

3. **Accessibility:**
    - o   Both rides are **wheelchair accessible**, and **single rider lines** are available for quicker access if you're okay riding alone.

4. **Keep Snacks Handy:**
    - o   Since both rides are full of fun and action, you might want a snack before or after. The **Krusty Burger** and **Lard Lad Donuts** near **The Simpsons Ride** and pet-themed snacks around **Secret Life of Pets** are a great way to fuel up.

The Simpsons Ride and **Secret Life of Pets: Off the Leash** are essential experiences at **Universal Studios Hollywood**, offering something for everyone—whether it's the zany fun of **Krustyland** with Homer and the gang or the heartwarming adventure through the pet world with Max and friends. With their combination of humor, thrilling action, and family-friendly fun, these attractions make the Upper Lot one of the most exciting areas in the park.

Lower Lot: Jurassic World: The Ride

Located in the **Lower Lot** of **Universal Studios Hollywood**, **Jurassic World: The Ride** is one of the park's most thrilling and awe-inspiring attractions. Based on the iconic **Jurassic Park** and **Jurassic World** franchises, this ride is a must-see for fans of dinosaurs and high-octane thrills. Here's everything you need to know about this jaw-dropping adventure.

Overview of Jurassic World: The Ride

Storyline:

In **Jurassic World: The Ride**, you enter the iconic **Jurassic World** theme park, where things have gone horribly wrong, and you're caught in the midst of a dangerous dinosaur escape. The ride immerses you in the world of massive, awe-inspiring dinosaurs and combines breathtaking animatronics, thrilling drops, and a heart-pounding water ride to create one of the most intense experiences in the park. The ride picks up the story where the **Jurassic World** movie left off, as the park is now open to visitors, but the dinosaurs are more dangerous than ever.

Ride Experience:

- **Pre-Ride Queue**:
  As you make your way through the **queue**, you'll feel the tension building, walking past a **futuristic control center** and viewing exhibits that give you a closer look at some of the dinosaurs. **Jurassic World's** cutting-edge technology is showcased, along with a glimpse into the behind-the-scenes operations, making you feel like you're really stepping into the park. Keep an eye out for some familiar elements from the **Jurassic World** films, such as the **Gyrosphere** ride and **Indominus rex containment area**.

- **The Ride Vehicle**:
  The ride takes place aboard a **dinosaur-themed boat**, which sets off on a water-filled journey through **Jurassic World**. You'll float past enclosures housing both **friendly** and **dangerous dinosaurs**, all brought to life using cutting-edge **animatronics** and **special effects**.
- **Thrilling Moments**:
    - **Giant Dinosaur Animatronics**: Encounter life-sized animatronic dinosaurs, such as the **Brachiosaurus**, **Triceratops**, and the terrifying **T. rex**, whose roars can shake you to the core. The detail of these creatures is astounding, making it feel like you're in the presence of real-life dinosaurs.
    - **The Indominus rex Encounter**: The heart-stopping part of the ride occurs when the **Indominus rex**, the genetically-engineered dinosaur from the movies, escapes from its pen, sending the park into chaos. The special effects and animatronics used to bring this creature to life are beyond impressive.
    - **The Big Drop**: Toward the end of the ride, the **Indominus rex** is on your tail as the boat makes an explosive **80-foot plunge** down a waterfall. This drop, coupled with the terrifying dinosaur encounter, makes for one of the most exhilarating parts of the experience.
    - **The Final Showdown**: As you make your escape, you'll come face-to-face with the enormous **T. rex**, who helps you narrowly escape the clutches of the **Indominus rex**. This final showdown is visually stunning, with enormous animatronics and water effects heightening the intensity of the experience.

Ride Highlights:

- **Life-Size Dinosaur Animatronics**: The ride features cutting-edge technology to bring dinosaurs to life in a way you've never seen before.
- **Surprise Encounters**: As you progress through the ride, expect unexpected dinosaur encounters that will keep you on the edge of your seat.
- **Thrilling Water Effects**: As a water-based ride, the final plunge and splashdown is one of the key features that makes this ride memorable.
- **Sound & Special Effects**: The sound effects, including the **roar of the T. rex** and the terrifying shrieks of the **Indominus rex**, heighten the intensity of the experience.

Pro Tips for Jurassic World: The Ride

1. **Prepare for a Thrill**:
   The ride features several intense moments, including a thrilling drop and encounters with dangerous dinosaurs. It's perfect for adrenaline junkies and **Jurassic World** fans but may be too intense for younger children or guests sensitive to motion.
2. **Age and Height Requirements**:
   Riders must be at least **42 inches tall** to ride, which makes it accessible for many kids, but be mindful of the ride's intensity when deciding if it's appropriate for your child.
3. **Wear Appropriate Clothing**:
   Given that this is a **water ride**, there's a good chance you'll get wet, especially toward the end of the ride during the big drop. Wear quick-drying clothes or bring a **poncho** to keep yourself dry.
4. **Avoid Getting Wet**:
   If you want to minimize the chances of getting wet, try sitting in the back of the boat, as the front tends to get more soaked

during the final splashdown. However, keep in mind that some water splashes may be unavoidable.

5. **Single Rider Line**:

   For quicker access, consider using the **single rider line** if you don't mind riding alone. This can be a huge time-saver during peak hours.

6. **Photo Opportunities**:

   Be on the lookout for **photo ops** at the ride's conclusion. While the photo might be taken during the final drop or dinosaur encounter, the photographers will capture your expression as you face down the **Indominus rex**.

Dining & Shopping Nearby

- **Jurassic   Café**:
  After experiencing the thrills of **Jurassic World: The Ride**, head over to **Jurassic Café**, which serves up a variety of hearty and flavorful meals in a **dinosaur-themed** setting. You'll find everything from burgers and salads to **dinosaur-themed snacks**, like **Velociraptor wings** and **Triceratops tacos**. Don't forget to try the **Dino Sweets** for a fun treat after your adventure.

- **The Jurassic Outfitters Shop**:
  Head to the **Jurassic Outfitters Shop** for all things **Jurassic World**. From **T. rex plush toys** and **Jurassic World T-shirts** to **hats, dinosaur figurines**, and **collectibles**, this store is a perfect place to grab a souvenir. You'll also find **official merchandise** based on the franchise, including apparel and accessories featuring your favorite dinosaurs.

Accessibility

- **Wheelchair Accessibility**: The ride is **wheelchair accessible**. There are designated areas for guests with mobility needs, ensuring everyone can enjoy the ride comfortably.

- **Rider Swap**: If you're visiting with a child who is unable to ride, take advantage of the **rider swap** program, where one guest can wait with the child while the rest of the party rides, and then swap places without having to wait in line again.

Jurassic World: The Ride is an epic, high-energy adventure that blends the thrills of **Jurassic World** with state-of-the-art animatronics, intense action, and incredible special effects. It's a must-ride for anyone who loves dinosaurs, adventure, and heart-pounding excitement. Whether you're a die-hard **Jurassic Park** fan or a newcomer to the franchise, this ride delivers an unforgettable experience that's sure to leave you talking long after you've exited the ride. From breathtaking visual effects to the terrifying encounters with prehistoric predators, **Jurassic World: The Ride** is a standout attraction in **Universal Studios Hollywood**.

Lower Lot: Transformers: The Ride 3D & Revenge of the Mummy: The Ride

Two of the most thrilling and visually spectacular rides in **Universal Studios Hollywood** are located in the **Lower Lot: Transformers: The Ride 3D** and **Revenge of the Mummy: The Ride**. Both attractions provide immersive experiences filled with cutting-edge technology, heart-racing moments, and cinematic storytelling. Let's break down each of these exciting rides in detail.

Transformers: The Ride 3D
Overview and Storyline
Transformers: The Ride 3D is a state-of-the-art, action-packed ride that immerses you in the battle between the Autobots and Decepticons. Based on the highly successful **Transformers** franchise, this ride lets you experience the excitement of the war between Optimus Prime's Autobots and Megatron's Decepticons in 3D.

- **Storyline**:
  The ride takes place in the **NEST** headquarters (a military base dedicated to protecting Earth from the Decepticons). As a member of the team, you're tasked with helping Optimus Prime and his Autobots prevent the Decepticons from obtaining the **AllSpark**, a powerful artifact that could give them ultimate power. You're thrust into an action-packed battle featuring high-speed chases, flying Decepticons, and devastating explosions as you help save the world from destruction.

- **Ride Experience**:
  - **3D Technology and Motion Simulation**: The ride utilizes **3D glasses** and **motion simulation** to create a fully immersive experience. You feel as though you're physically being thrown into the action as your ride

vehicle shakes, tilts, and moves in sync with the on-screen battle.

- o **Special Effects and Set Design**: From the explosive action sequences to the intricate set design, the ride uses special effects like **flames**, **water spray**, and **air blasts** to create a truly dynamic environment. You'll feel every crash, rumble, and explosion as if you're right in the middle of the battle.
- o **Transformers Characters**: The ride features all the iconic **Transformers** characters, including **Optimus Prime**, **Bumblebee**, **Megatron**, and **Starscream**, brought to life through **3D projections** and **giant animatronics**.
- o **Action-Packed Battle**: As the ride progresses, you'll find yourself in intense action sequences, including battles in the streets of **Chicago**, fighting off Decepticons as they attempt to steal the **AllSpark**.

Ride Highlights:

- **Immersive 3D Battle**: Feel the adrenaline rush as you're placed in the heart of the Autobots' battle against the Decepticons.
- **Next-Level Animation and Visuals**: The 3D visuals are stunning, offering breathtaking sequences where you come face-to-face with massive **Transformers**.
- **Action & Motion**: The motion-based elements, combined with 3D technology, make you feel like you're right there with the Autobots, dodging attacks, avoiding falling debris, and experiencing the thrill of the chase.
- **Sound & Effects**: The ride's surround sound system and special effects create a truly cinematic experience, making you feel as though you're on a real battlefield.

Pro Tips:

- **For Thrill-Seekers**: If you love intense action and fast-paced thrills, this ride is for you. The combination of high-speed motions and visual effects makes it one of the most adrenaline-pumping attractions at the park.
- **Get There Early**: Transformers: The Ride 3D is one of the most popular attractions in the park, so head to it early in the day or later in the evening to avoid long lines.
- **Age & Height Requirements**: Riders must be at least **40 inches tall** to ride. The ride is suitable for children and adults, but be aware that it's a fast-paced, intense experience.

Nearby Dining & Shopping:

- **Transformers Gift Shop**: After the ride, visit the **Transformers store** to find **action figures, apparel,** and other merchandise featuring your favorite **Transformers** characters.
- **AllSpark Café**: Stop by this themed café for quick snacks or meals before or after your adventure. Grab a **Transformer-themed drink** or **snack** to fuel up for more fun.

Revenge of the Mummy: The Ride

Overview and Storyline

Revenge of the Mummy: The Ride is an indoor roller coaster that combines high-speed thrills with terrifying special effects and elements of the **Mummy** franchise. This ride is a thrilling mix of a **dark ride, coaster,** and **interactive experience**.

- **Storyline**:
  The ride is set in the world of **The Mummy** movies, specifically the **Mummy Returns** storyline. You begin your journey in the **Mummy's tomb**, where you're greeted by the ancient Egyptian mummy **Imhotep**, who seeks to punish anyone who dares enter his cursed lair. The ride quickly escalates into an adrenaline-pumping roller coaster as you face

off against **mummies, fire**, and even **dark magic** as you attempt to escape **Imhotep's curse**.

- **Ride Experience**:
  - o **The Dark Ride Begins**: You first enter the **ancient Egyptian tomb**, encountering eerie lighting, tombs, and relics from the world of the **Mummy**. As you make your way through the dark, **haunted corridors**, you come face-to-face with **Imhotep**, whose vengeful curse is unleashed.
  - o **The Thrilling Roller Coaster**: Just when you think you're safe, the ride quickly turns into a **roller coaster**. You'll experience sudden drops, high-speed twists, and surprises at every turn, all while racing through the **Mummy's lair**. The coaster elements are intense, but the surprises come from the eerie set pieces and special effects that make you feel like you're being chased by the **Mummy**.
  - o **Special Effects**: From **fire bursts** and **air blasts** to **animatronic mummies** and intense sound effects, the ride creates a heart-pounding experience. The combination of physical ride elements and visual effects adds a terrifying edge to the roller coaster.

Ride Highlights:

- **Fast-Paced Roller Coaster**: The ride features **high-speed coaster elements**, such as sharp turns and sudden drops, all set in a dark, eerie environment.
- **Mummy Animatronics**: As you race through the tombs, you'll encounter terrifying **mummy animatronics**, which seem to spring to life and chase after you.
- **Fire and Special Effects**: Watch as **fire** erupts around you and **magic** seems to come alive, creating a truly terrifying atmosphere as the ride moves at breakneck speeds.

- **Intense Thrills**: The ride is known for its **surprise twists**, sudden launches, and the unexpected **reverse drop**, which makes it a thrilling experience from start to finish.

Pro Tips:
- **Not for the Faint of Heart**: If you're looking for a roller coaster with thrills, scares, and surprises, this ride is perfect. However, if you're sensitive to **dark environments** or intense experiences, this ride may be a bit much.
- **Age & Height Requirements**: Riders must be at least **48 inches tall** to ride. This ride is ideal for older kids and adults who love thrilling roller coasters with a spooky twist.
- **Get Ready for Surprises**: The **reverse drop** and sudden coaster elements can catch you off guard, so be prepared for a heart-racing ride that's full of twists and turns.

Nearby Dining & Shopping:
- **Revenge of the Mummy Gift Shop**: After you survive the ride, stop by the **Mummy gift shop** for **Mummy-themed merchandise**, including action figures, jewelry, and collectibles inspired by the movies.
- **Themed Snacks**: While there are no dedicated restaurants around the ride, you'll find themed snacks and refreshments at nearby carts and shops throughout the **Lower Lot**.

Both **Transformers: The Ride 3D** and **Revenge of the Mummy: The Ride** offer some of the most exciting, intense, and visually stunning experiences at **Universal Studios Hollywood**. From high-speed chases through the **Transformers universe** to escaping the curse of **Imhotep's mummy** in a thrilling indoor roller coaster, these attractions provide unforgettable moments for anyone who loves action, adventure, and immersive storytelling. Whether you're a fan of the **Transformers** franchise or enjoy classic horror thrills, these rides are bound to make your visit to the park even more memorable.

Studio Tour: Behind the Scenes of Classic and Modern Film Sets

The **Studio Tour** at **Universal Studios Hollywood** is one of the park's most iconic attractions, offering a behind-the-scenes glimpse into the world of film production. Whether you're a movie buff or simply enjoy seeing the magic of filmmaking come to life, this guided tour takes you through **classic** and **modern film sets**, providing an unforgettable experience.

Overview of the Studio Tour

The **Studio Tour** is a **50-minute** guided ride through **Universal Studios Hollywood's working film lot**. This tour offers an exclusive look at some of the world's most famous film sets, soundstages, and backlot areas, where classic films and the latest blockbusters come to life. You'll have the chance to see where some of your favorite movies and TV shows were made, as well as experience the tools and techniques filmmakers use to create cinematic magic.

The tour is hosted on **open-air trams** and is led by **knowledgeable guides** who share interesting facts, trivia, and stories about the productions that have taken place on the lot over the years. You'll see the evolution of filmmaking, from **classic Universal Studios films** to the high-tech productions of today.

What to Expect on the Studio Tour

Classic Film Sets

The **Studio Tour** includes stops at some of **Universal's most iconic and timeless film sets**, where you'll feel like you've stepped right into your favorite **classic movies**. Here are just a few examples of what you may encounter on the tour:

- **King Kong 360 3D**:
  This is one of the most thrilling moments on the Studio Tour. You'll come face-to-face with **King Kong**, brought to life

through **3D projection technology** and stunning special effects. As the tram makes its way through the set, King Kong comes to life in a battle with a **T-Rex**, creating a heart-pounding, 360-degree experience. The intense visual effects and motion simulation make you feel as if you're in the middle of the action.

- **The Psycho House**:
  A stop at the **Psycho House** takes you to the iconic home from **Alfred Hitchcock's Psycho**, one of the most famous horror films in history. You can see the eerie **mansion** and the **infamous Bates Motel**, where the famous shower scene was filmed. This set is a must-see for fans of classic cinema and film history.

- **The Desperate Housewives Set**:
  The charming, suburban streets of **Wisteria Lane**, the setting of the hit TV show **Desperate Housewives**, are another highlight. As you cruise down this **iconic set**, you'll recognize many of the homes and backyards where the drama, laughter, and intrigue unfolded in the series.

- **The Fast & Furious: Supercharged**:
  Experience a high-octane, high-speed adventure with **Fast & Furious: Supercharged**. This part of the tour gives you an up-close look at some of the cars and sets used in the **Fast & Furious franchise**, and it even takes you on an exciting tram ride where you become part of the action in a thrilling, high-speed chase.

Modern Film Sets

While classic sets certainly dominate the tour, the **Studio Tour** also gives you access to **modern** sets that highlight the cutting-edge technology used in today's blockbuster films. These are some of the modern film-making innovations that make Universal Studios stand out:

- **Soundstages and Sets for Modern Films**:
  As you venture through the backlot, your guide may show you current film **sets** being used for major productions. Depending on the day, you could pass by the **sets** of films like **Jurassic World, The Walking Dead**, or **Fast & Furious**. Universal Studios has been home to numerous blockbuster franchises over the years, and you may catch a glimpse of some of the latest productions in progress.
- **Special Effects Demonstrations**:
  On the Studio Tour, you'll have the chance to experience the cutting-edge special effects that bring **modern films** to life. This includes **live demonstrations** of **water explosions, fire effects**, and **robotic props** used in the making of action-packed films. You'll gain a new appreciation for the work that goes into creating seamless, thrilling movie magic.
- **The Wizarding World of Harry Potter (Hogwarts Castle)**:
  While the **Wizarding World of Harry Potter** is a fully immersive attraction in its own right, parts of its incredible set can be seen during the Studio Tour. You'll pass by a model of **Hogwarts Castle, Hogsmeade**, and other key locations from the **Harry Potter** films. The level of detail and design in the set is staggering, making it a highlight for fans of the franchise.

The Universal Backlot

The **backlot** is one of the most exciting places to explore during the Studio Tour. It's home to numerous **film sets**, both real and replicated, and it's where countless famous films and TV shows have been shot. Here are some of the locations you may pass through:

- **New York Street**:
  The **New York Street** set is one of the most famous backlot locations. With its **replica buildings**, streets, and alleyways, it's been used in many productions, from **Spider-Man** films to **Desperate Housewives**. It's a versatile set that can be re-dressed to look like any urban city, and you'll often see it in

the background of action sequences or as the location for major scenes in films.

- **Courthouse Square (Back to the Future)**: Fans of **Back to the Future** will be thrilled to visit **Courthouse Square**, the filming location for the iconic **Clock Tower** scene from the film. You'll get a chance to see the **town square** and the **DeLorean** time machine up close, immersing yourself in one of cinema's most beloved time-travel tales.
- **Wisteria Lane**: Fans of the hit TV show **Desperate Housewives** will recognize the familiar homes and streets of **Wisteria Lane**. It's one of the most recognizable sets on the lot, and a stroll down the street gives you a taste of suburban drama in all its glory.

Studio Tour Highlights
- **Interactive Elements**: Throughout the tour, you'll be guided by a knowledgeable host who will provide interesting facts, fun behind-the-scenes stories, and trivia about the films shot on the lot. It's an entertaining way to learn more about the world of filmmaking.
- **Exclusive Access**: The Studio Tour offers exclusive access to **working film sets** and soundstages, which you won't find anywhere else. You'll feel like a part of the action as you travel through some of the most famous sets in cinematic history.
- **Cinematic Experiences**: Besides the behind-the-scenes sets, you'll experience cinematic action with special effects, such as the **King Kong 360 3D** encounter and the **Fast & Furious: Supercharged**

segment. These effects immerse you in the thrill of action-packed films, making you feel like you're part of the movie.

Pro Tips for the Studio Tour
1. **Check for Filming Schedules**:
   The Studio Tour takes you through active film sets, so it's a good idea to check ahead to see if any major productions are filming during your visit. Some areas may be closed for filming, and it can affect the experience.
2. **Plan to Arrive Early**:
   The Studio Tour is a popular attraction, so arrive early in the day to avoid long wait times. It's also a great way to start your visit, as it gives you an overview of the entire park.
3. **Bring Sunscreen and Comfortable Shoes**:
   The tour takes place outdoors, and you'll be driving through different parts of the studio lot. Bring **sunscreen**, **sunglasses**, and comfortable walking shoes, as you may have to walk short distances to access the tour vehicle.
4. **Age and Height Requirements**:
   The Studio Tour is suitable for all ages, with no height restrictions. It's a fun and educational experience for both children and adults.

The **Studio Tour** at **Universal Studios Hollywood** is a must-do experience for anyone visiting the park. With its combination of **classic film sets**, **modern productions**, and behind-the-scenes access, it provides a unique and immersive look into the world of filmmaking. Whether you're a fan of **classic cinema**, a lover of special effects, or simply curious about how movies are made, the Studio Tour offers something for everyone. It's an unforgettable journey that will make you feel like you've stepped into the world of your favorite films.

King Kong 360 3D & Fast & Furious – Supercharged: Thrilling Experiences at Universal Studios Hollywood

Two of the most thrilling and action-packed experiences at **Universal Studios Hollywood** are **King Kong 360 3D** and **Fast & Furious – Supercharged**. Both attractions are known for their breathtaking special effects, immersive storytelling, and high-energy action. Here's a detailed guide to what you can expect from these two unforgettable rides.

King Kong 360 3D: Face-to-Face with a Movie Icon

Overview

King Kong 360 3D is a visually stunning, heart-pounding experience that immerses you in the world of the legendary giant ape. This ride is one of the highlights of the **Studio Tour**, and it brings the iconic creature to life using state-of-the-art **3D technology** and **special effects**.

You'll experience **King Kong 360 3D** during your journey through the **backlot** on the **Studio Tour** tram ride. The ride takes place in a **purpose-built soundstage** where you'll find yourself in the middle of a massive battle between **King Kong** and a rampaging **T-Rex**. This attraction is a mix of a traditional **dark ride**, immersive **3D visuals**, and **motion simulation**.

Storyline

As you move through the set, you'll find yourself in the middle of an epic battle for survival. The tram ride takes you into a dangerous jungle environment, where the tram is suddenly ambushed by a pack of wild, monstrous creatures. You'll witness King Kong, the mighty ape, engage in a fierce battle with a **T-Rex**, trying to protect you from danger. The interaction between Kong and the T-Rex is brought to life through **3D projection technology**, making it feel as though you're right there with them.

- **The Battle**: The most thrilling moment comes when King Kong faces off with a **Tyrannosaurus Rex**. As you look around, you'll see **King Kong's massive hands** coming closer, and you'll feel the **earthquake-like tremors** of the beast's movements. The **T-Rex** lunges toward you, and you'll be engulfed in a terrifying, action-packed sequence that feels truly cinematic.
- **The Special Effects**: The ride uses **motion simulation, 3D projections**, and **surround sound** to bring the action to life. **Air blasts, water sprays**, and **flying debris** make the experience even more immersive, making you feel like you're in the middle of a monster movie.

Key Features
- **3D Technology**: The 3D visuals are stunning, with **King Kong** and the **T-Rex** appearing as massive, lifelike creatures. The detailed textures and animations make the experience incredibly realistic.
- **Motion Simulation**: As you ride the tram, you'll feel the action all around you. The tram moves in sync with the battle, tilting and swaying as you dodge attacks and watch Kong fight off the T-Rex.
- **Sensory Effects**: The ride also uses **air blasts, water mist**, and even the **smell of the jungle** to make the experience as immersive as possible.

Pro Tips
- **Height and Age Requirements**: There are no specific height requirements, but the

attraction is suitable for guests of all ages, including children. However, it might be intense for younger kids due to the frightening nature of the visuals and sounds.

- **Best Time to Visit**: This ride is part of the Studio Tour, which is one of the most popular attractions at the park. To avoid long wait times, plan to ride it early in the day or later in the afternoon.

Fast & Furious – Supercharged: An Adrenaline-Fueled Thrill Ride
Overview

If you're a fan of high-speed car chases and over-the-top action, **Fast & Furious – Supercharged** is the ride for you. This **motion-based simulation ride** takes you into the heart of the **Fast & Furious** franchise, where you'll team up with characters from the films for an action-packed chase sequence. As part of the **Studio Tour**, this attraction uses **4K technology**, **motion simulation**, and **3D visuals** to put you right in the middle of a **high-speed pursuit**.
Storyline

In **Fast & Furious – Supercharged**, you join **Dominic Toretto** (played by **Vin Diesel**) and his crew in a high-octane chase to rescue a key witness and stop a criminal syndicate from taking over. You'll jump into the action, where you're pursued by enemy vehicles, dodging explosions, speeding through streets, and trying to escape from dangerous situations at every turn.

- **The Action**: The ride begins as you're introduced to the **Fast & Furious crew** who brief you on the mission. From there, you're thrown into a thrilling chase, with **cars speeding by**, helicopters overhead, and **explosions** all around. It's an action-packed journey where you're constantly trying to evade capture by the enemy.

- **The Car Chase**: At the heart of the ride is a wild car chase. You'll feel the speed and intensity of the pursuit as you race through the streets of **Los Angeles**, narrowly avoiding obstacles and escaping enemy vehicles.

Key Features

- **Advanced Special Effects**: Fast & Furious – **Supercharged** makes use of some of the most advanced special effects available. The ride utilizes **4K projection, motion simulators**, and **physical effects** like **wind, flashes of light**, and **sound** to make the experience as immersive as possible.

- **High-Speed Chase**: The ride itself feels like a fast-paced car chase, with **sharp turns**, **quick accelerations**, and dramatic slow-motion sequences. You'll feel as if you're in a car chase from the movies.

- **Live Action**: The experience also includes **live-action elements** where you encounter characters from the **Fast & Furious** franchise, including **Vin Diesel** and **Paul Walker** (via projections). The interactions help build excitement and make you feel like a part of the action.

Pro Tips

- **Height and Age Requirements**: Riders must be at least **40 inches tall** to ride. While the ride isn't physically intense, it can be overwhelming due to the speed and excitement of the car chase.

- **Not for the Faint of Heart**: If you love **action**, **explosions**, and **high-speed thrills**, this is a must-see. However, if you're sensitive to sudden movements or fast motion, you might want to skip this one.

- **Best Time to Visit**: Like **King Kong 360 3D, Fast & Furious – Supercharged** is part of the **Studio Tour**, so you'll want to plan to get on the ride early or later in the day to avoid peak times.

Key Differences: King Kong 360 3D vs. Fast & Furious – Supercharged

Feature	King Kong 360 3D	Fast & Furious – Supercharged
Type of Ride	3D motion-simulation dark ride	High-speed car chase motion simulator
Storyline	Battle between King Kong and a T-Rex	A thrilling chase through Los Angeles to rescue a witness
Main Attraction	3D projection of King Kong fighting a T-Rex	Fast-paced car chase with explosions and action scenes
Special Effects	3D projections, motion simulation, air blasts	4K projections, motion simulators, wind, lights, and sound
Intensity	Moderate to high thrill, but not too intense	High thrill with intense motion and high-speed elements
Best for	Fans of King Kong and monster movies	Fans of the Fast & Furious franchise and car chases

Both **King Kong 360 3D** and **Fast & Furious – Supercharged** are immersive, high-energy rides that deliver unique experiences at **Universal Studios Hollywood**. Whether you're facing a gigantic King Kong in a jungle battle or zooming through a high-speed car chase, these rides offer exhilarating thrills, impressive special effects, and unforgettable moments. If you love **action**, **special effects**, and **cinematic experiences**, these two attractions are not to be missed during your visit to the park.

Live Shows and Entertainment: WaterWorld – A Live Sea War Spectacular

WaterWorld: A Live Sea War Spectacular is one of the most thrilling and action-packed live shows at **Universal Studios Hollywood**, offering visitors a chance to see **live stunts, explosive effects**, and **high-flying action** right before their eyes. Based on the 1995 cult-classic movie **Waterworld**, this show has become a fan favorite over the years, combining **water-based stunts**, **explosions**, and **dramatic performances** to deliver a truly unforgettable experience.

Here's everything you need to know about this **spectacular live show** that combines all the excitement of a blockbuster action film with the thrill of a live performance.

WaterWorld: A Live Sea War Spectacular
At **WaterWorld**, the action takes place on a **massive open-air stage** filled with water, fire, and **aerial stunts**, creating a dramatic backdrop for an epic battle of survival. The show combines **live performances** with **advanced special effects**, including **fire**

explosions, **water jets**, and **motorized stunt boats**, ensuring that there's never a dull moment.

The show's **storyline** is inspired by the **Waterworld movie**, set in a post-apocalyptic future where the Earth has been flooded, and the remaining human survivors live on makeshift floating cities. The show's plot follows a group of **survivors** as they battle pirates and face dangerous obstacles in a desperate attempt to survive.

The Storyline: Survival in a Flooded World

The show begins with an introduction to a **dystopian future** where the seas have swallowed most of the land. The remnants of humanity have turned to floating islands and makeshift ships to survive. The central **hero** of the show is a lone **drifter** known only as the **Mariner**, who navigates this dangerous world.

A group of pirates known as the **Smokers** have seized control of the waters, terrorizing survivors and looking for a mysterious map that leads to the **Dryland**, a fabled paradise where the Earth's surface is still habitable. The **Mariner** gets caught in a battle between the **Smokers** and a group of survivors who have taken refuge on a floating atoll.

- **The Mariner**: The main hero of the show, a rugged and mysterious drifter, represents the last hope for the survivors.
- **The Smokers**: The villainous pirate crew, led by a ruthless commander, who will stop at nothing to find Dryland and control the remaining resources.
- **The Survivors**: A group of resilient people who are trying to protect the secrets of **Dryland** from the Smokers and escape the post-apocalyptic chaos.

Throughout the show, the action intensifies as the **Mariner** and the survivors face off against the **Smokers** in a **water-based battle** full of explosions, stunts, and high-speed boat chases. The **fighting, chase sequences**, and **aerial stunts** keep the audience at the edge of their seats as they experience firsthand the dangers of this flooded world.

What to Expect During the Show

WaterWorld: A Live Sea War Spectacular is packed with jaw-dropping special effects, live action, and stunts that make it one of the most exciting live performances at **Universal Studios Hollywood**. Here are some of the standout features of the show:

Aerial Stunts

- **High-flying action** is a major part of the show. Stunt performers launch themselves off platforms, using **ropes** and **harnesses** to perform **death-defying dives** into the water below.
- Watch as actors **leap off structures** and **dangle from ropes**, providing gravity-defying moments that add excitement to the show.
- The aerial stunts also include **high-speed jet skis** and **airborne acrobatics**, as the performers battle both in the air and on the water.

Water-Based Action

- As the show takes place on a **floating stage**, the **water** itself becomes a key player in the action. Expect **waterfalls, splash effects**, and **massive waves** to be a part of the show's most dramatic moments.
- **Jet skis** zoom across the stage, performing **high-speed chases** that lead to thrilling collisions and explosive stunts.
- One of the most exciting aspects of the show is the **huge water explosions** that send **massive waves** crashing over the stage, soaking the actors and sometimes the audience.

Explosions and Fire Effects

- Throughout the performance, you'll witness **massive explosions** that light up the sky, accompanied by **flames** shooting out of props and boats. The pyrotechnics are a major highlight of the show, providing a stunning visual display.
- **Fire effects** are used to create chaos, with **flames** shooting from boats and other props as part of the battle between the Smokers and the survivors.

Stunt Boats and Jet Skis

- **Stunt boats** play a central role in the action, as they race across the water, perform **high-speed turns**, and even **flip** over in daring stunts. These boats are **motorized** and custom-designed to perform complex tricks during the show.
- **Jet skis** are also used extensively, adding to the **high-speed chases** and **aerial stunts**, as the actors zip across the water and perform dramatic flips and turns.

Live Performances and Combat

- **Hand-to-hand combat** is a major part of the show, as the **Mariner** faces off against the **Smokers** in a series of **high-intensity fights**. The **stunt actors** are highly trained, and their fight sequences are expertly choreographed, giving the show an authentic action-movie feel.
- The **performers** interact with the audience as part of the show, sometimes even engaging in dramatic sequences that place them close to the crowd, creating a sense of excitement and danger.

Key Features

- **Massive Stage**: The **WaterWorld** stage is one of the largest live-action performance spaces in the park, measuring over **3 acres** in size. The stage itself is made up of a **floating platform** and **water tanks**, allowing for the dynamic water effects that are so central to the performance.

- **Advanced Special Effects**: From **explosive blasts** to **water jets, fire effects,** and **flying stunt performers**, the show is packed with high-tech effects that bring the post-apocalyptic world to life.
- **Trained Stunt Performers**: The action is all performed by highly skilled stuntmen and women, whose expertise makes each performance a thrilling spectacle. Many of the performers in **WaterWorld** are seasoned professionals, with backgrounds in film and television stunt work.

Pro Tips for Watching WaterWorld: A Live Sea War Spectacular
1. **Seating**: There are a variety of seating options available for **WaterWorld**, and some sections of the theater offer a better view than others. For the best experience, try to sit in the **center** of the audience, or consider sitting in the **"soak zone"** for a chance to get splashed by the explosive water effects.
2. **Arrive Early**: The show is very popular, so arriving early can help you get a better seat. Also, arriving early allows you to choose between seating in the **dry zone** or the **soak zone**, depending on how much you want to be immersed in the action.
3. **Prepare to Get Wet**: If you want to be at the front, or in the **soak zone**, be prepared to get splashed! The effects can be pretty intense, especially during the water explosions and high-speed boat chases.
4. **Check the Show Times**: **WaterWorld** runs multiple times throughout the day, but showtimes may vary depending on the park's schedule. Be sure to check the times when you arrive at the park, as some shows might be cancelled due to weather or other unforeseen factors.
5. **The Soak Zone**: For those who love the thrill of getting drenched, head straight for the **soak zone**. Just be prepared

with **extra clothes** or a **poncho** if you don't want to spend the rest of the day wet!

WaterWorld: A Live Sea War Spectacular is a must-see attraction at **Universal Studios Hollywood** that combines **action**, **drama**, and **spectacular effects** into an unforgettable live show. Whether you're a fan of the movie or simply love thrilling live entertainment, this show offers something for everyone. From **aerial stunts** to **explosive pyrotechnics**, it's an experience you'll never forget. So grab a seat, brace yourself for the splash, and get ready for a **thrill ride** like no other!

Special Effects Show & Character Meet-and-Greets at Universal Studios Hollywood

Universal Studios Hollywood is known for its world-class **special effects** and opportunities to meet iconic characters from some of the biggest movies and franchises in history. Two key features of the park are the **Special Effects Show** and the **Character Meet-and-Greets**, which offer guests the chance to dive deeper into the magic of movie-making and interact with beloved characters in a fun and engaging way.

Special Effects Show: Behind the Magic of Movies
Overview of the Special Effects Show
The **Special Effects Show** is a live, interactive experience that gives visitors an insider's look at how movie magic is made. Hosted by Universal Studios Hollywood's talented special effects team, the show is filled with exciting demonstrations, fascinating behind-the-scenes secrets, and jaw-dropping effects. It's the perfect attraction for those interested in the technical side of film production.

What to Expect in the Special Effects Show
The show walks you through several different aspects of creating a blockbuster film, including visual effects, sound effects, stunt work, and more. Expect to see a variety of **live demonstrations** and **practical effects**, along with an inside look at how some of your favorite scenes are created.

- **Live Demonstrations**: The show will demonstrate how various special effects are achieved, including how explosions are created, how stunt work is performed, and how CGI (computer-generated imagery) is used to enhance movies. Some of these demonstrations are interactive, so you may be called up to help create a movie effect.

- **Stunt Performances**: Watch as trained stunt performers demonstrate techniques used in action films, such as how **high falls** are safely executed or how **fire stunts** are managed.
- **Sound and Visual Effects**: Learn how movie soundtracks and effects like footsteps, background sounds, and explosions are created using everyday items or high-tech tools. You'll see how sound effects are recorded and synchronized to picture.
- **How CGI is Used**: Get a sneak peek at how **CGI** transforms movie scenes. Whether it's turning an ordinary object into something larger than life or creating entire fantasy worlds, the show will demonstrate how these amazing visual effects are accomplished.

Show Highlights
- **Interactive Experiences**: Some of the demonstrations allow guests to interact with the special effects team to help create explosions or add sound effects to a film scene. This interactive aspect makes the show fun and educational.
- **Hollywood Secrets**: The show reveals **behind-the-scenes tricks** that even the most seasoned moviegoers may not know. How do they make creatures appear life-like? How do filmmakers create a realistic fight scene? These questions and more are answered during the show.
- **Stunning Visuals**: From explosive

pyrotechnics to cool visual effects, the Special Effects Show provides an all-encompassing cinematic experience that shows the real power of film technology.

Tips for Attending the Special Effects Show

- **Show Times**: The **Special Effects Show** runs multiple times throughout the day. Be sure to check the daily schedule upon entering the park for the exact times. The schedule can vary, especially during peak seasons, so planning ahead will ensure you don't miss it.
- **Arrive Early**: Seating for the Special Effects Show can fill up quickly, especially during busy periods. Arriving a few minutes before showtime ensures you get a good seat with an excellent view of the demonstrations.
- **Age and Intensity**: The show is appropriate for all ages. It does feature some loud noises and flashes of light, so be aware if you're sensitive to such effects, but it is family-friendly and entertaining for kids and adults alike.
- **Location**: The **Special Effects Show** is located in the **Lower Lot** of the park, so be prepared to head down to this section after entering the park.

Character Meet-and-Greets: Meet Your Favorite Stars
One of the most exciting parts of any visit to **Universal Studios Hollywood** is the chance to meet beloved characters from movies and TV shows. Whether you're a fan of **Minions**, **The Simpsons**, **Marvel superheroes**, or the iconic

Universal monsters, the park offers a variety of **meet-and-greet experiences** that let you take a photo and interact with your favorite characters.

Where to Meet Characters

Character meet-and-greets are spread throughout the park, and you can meet characters in designated areas, such as:

- **Upper Lot**: Here you'll find popular characters from **Despicable Me**, **The Simpsons**, and **Jurassic Park**, among others.
- **Lower Lot**: You'll encounter characters like **Transformers** robots and **Minions** in this area.
- **In Front of the Studio Tour**: Some characters are available for photos in front of the iconic **studio entrance**.

Popular Character Meet-and-Greets

Here are some of the most popular characters you can meet in **Universal Studios Hollywood**:

- **Minions** (Despicable Me): These mischievous, yellow creatures are always a crowd favorite. You can find them in the **Upper Lot**, where you can interact with them for some photo ops and plenty of laughs.
- **Transformers Characters**: **Optimus Prime** and **Bumblebee** are usually found in the **Lower Lot**, posing for photos with guests in their full **robotic gear**. These life-sized robots are incredible to see up close.
- **The Simpsons**: You'll meet **Homer, Marge, Bart, Lisa**, and **Maggie** from the iconic animated series in **Springfield**. The Simpsons area offers a

chance to take a picture with the whole family and enjoy some fun, lighthearted interaction.

- **Marvel Superheroes**: **Spider-Man**, **Captain America**, **Iron Man**, and other Marvel superheroes can be found in the **Upper Lot**, especially around the Marvel area. They're always ready for a quick chat and photo opportunity.
- **The Mummy & Jurassic Park**: Characters from the **Mummy** series and the **Jurassic Park** films occasionally make appearances for meet-and-greet moments, allowing you to take pictures with **Jurassic World** raptors or **Imhotep** from the Mummy franchise.
- **Universal Monsters**: Meet the classic **Frankenstein monster**, **The**

Wolfman, **The Bride of Frankenstein**, and **Dracula** in the Universal Monsters area. These larger-than-life characters are ready to pose for spooky photos.

Tips for Meet-and-Greets

- **Check the Schedule**: Character appearances can vary throughout the day. Be sure to check the **daily schedule** to see when and where your favorite characters will be making their appearances. These times are posted around the park and on the Universal Studios Hollywood app.
- **Get in Line Early**: Popular characters like **Minions** or **Transformers** can have long lines, especially during busy times. To maximize your chances of

meeting them, it's best to get in line early.

- **Take Photos**: Don't forget to bring your camera or phone to take pictures! Most character meet-and-greet sessions include **photo ops**, and the actors will often strike fun poses for your photos.
- **Autographs**: While autographs are not always guaranteed, some characters will offer autographs upon request. Bring a piece of memorabilia or just ask them politely for an autograph.
- **Interactive Experiences**: Some characters engage with guests, making the experience more personal and interactive. Whether it's a quick chat, a silly pose, or a special handshake, you can often enjoy some unique moments with these larger-than-life characters.
- **Character Guidelines**: Some characters, such as **Transformers robots**, may require you to stand at a certain distance due to the **complex costume** or **robot mechanics**. Be sure to follow any guidelines set by the performers to ensure everyone's safety and enjoyment.

Directions to the Special Effects Show & Character Meet-and-Greets

- **To the Special Effects Show**:
  - The **Special Effects Show** is located in the **Lower Lot** of Universal Studios Hollywood. After entering the park and passing through the **Upper Lot**,

head down the escalators or take the **tram** to the **Lower Lot**. The show's entrance is well-marked, and you'll find signs directing you to it once you reach the Lower Lot.

To the Character Meet-and-Greets:

Character meet-and-greet locations are spread throughout the park. The **Upper Lot** has several meet-and-greet areas near **The Simpsons** and **Despicable Me** attractions. The **Lower Lot** is home to **Transformers** and **Minions** character meet-ups.

Be sure to check the daily schedule, as characters may move to different locations depending on the day's itinerary and special events.

Both the **Special Effects Show** and **Character Meet-and-Greets** at **Universal Studios Hollywood** provide guests with opportunities to experience the magic of movie-making up close and personal. Whether you're watching **behind-the-scenes special effects** come to life or meeting some of your favorite movie characters, these attractions offer unique, interactive experiences that are fun for all ages. Be sure to take full advantage of both attractions to make your visit to Universal Studios Hollywood even more memorable!

Cindy Bear & Yoki Bear

CHAPTER 6

Dining and Snacks at Universal Studios Hollywood: Dining Guide by Area

Whether you're craving a quick snack to keep you energized throughout the day or looking for a sit-down meal to relax and recharge, Universal Studios Hollywood offers a variety of dining options to suit all tastes and preferences. From quick bites to full-course meals, there's something for everyone, no matter how much time you have or what kind of food you're in the mood for.

In this guide, we'll walk you through the dining options by area—helping you navigate where to find the best quick bites and sit-down meals across the park.

Dining in the Upper Lot

The **Upper Lot** is home to some of the most iconic attractions in the park, and it's also where you'll find a range of dining options. Whether you're looking for a fast snack or a more leisurely meal, the Upper Lot has something to satisfy your cravings.

Quick Bites:

1. **Mel's Diner**
   - **Location**: Upper Lot, next to the **Transformers** attraction.
   - **Cuisine**: Classic American diner food.
   - **Must-Try**: Mel's famous **burger and fries**, **milkshakes**.
   - **Overview**: For a quick and satisfying bite, Mel's Diner serves up traditional diner fare like burgers, fries, and milkshakes. It's a great spot for families or anyone looking to grab a quick bite in a retro, 50s-inspired environment.

2. **Cletus' Chicken Shack**
   - **Location**: Springfield, near **Krustyland**.
   - **Cuisine**: Fried chicken and fast food.
   - **Must-Try**: **Fried chicken tenders**, **corn on the cob**, and **Krusty's famous chicken sandwiches**.
   - **Overview**: Located in **Springfield**, this quick-service spot offers hearty portions of fried chicken, sandwiches, and sides. It's perfect for a casual, quick meal before heading back to your next ride.

3. **Lard Lad Donuts**
   - **Location**: Springfield, near **Krusty's Burger**.
   - **Cuisine**: Donuts and sweet snacks.
   - **Must-Try**: **Giant Lard Lad donut, mini donuts**.
   - **Overview**: Don't miss the opportunity to grab a sweet treat at **Lard Lad Donuts**. The famous **giant donut** is a perfect snack to enjoy while you wander through

Springfield. They also offer smaller-sized donuts for an easy grab-and-go option.

Sit-Down Meals:

1. **The Three Broomsticks**
   - **Location**: The **Wizarding World of Harry Potter**.
   - **Cuisine**: British pub fare, inspired by the Harry Potter films.
   - **Must-Try**: **Fish and chips**, **shepherd's pie**, and **Butterbeer**.
   - **Overview**: This immersive pub-style restaurant is set inside the **Wizarding World of Harry Potter** and offers hearty British dishes like fish and chips, shepherd's pie, and roast chicken. Be sure to try **Butterbeer**, a must-have for any Harry Potter fan.

2. **Bubba Gump Shrimp Co.**
   - **Location**: Upper Lot, near the **WaterWorld**.
   - **Cuisine**: Seafood and Southern-inspired dishes.
   - **Must-Try**: **Shrimp dishes**, **Cajun shrimp**, and **seafood platters**.
   - **Overview**: Inspired by the **Forrest Gump** movie, **Bubba Gump Shrimp Co.** offers a full sit-down experience with a variety of seafood and Southern-inspired dishes. From fried shrimp to **Cajun-style** platters, this restaurant is ideal for seafood lovers looking for a more relaxed meal.

Dining in the Lower Lot

The **Lower Lot** houses some of Universal Studios Hollywood's most thrilling rides, but it also offers a variety of dining options to help fuel you throughout the day.

Quick Bites:
1. **Jurassic Cafe**
   - **Location**: Lower Lot, near **Jurassic World: The Ride**.
   - **Cuisine**: American comfort food.
   - **Must-Try**: **Ribs, pulled pork sandwiches**, and **dino-shaped chicken nuggets**.
   - **Overview**: If you're spending time in **Jurassic World**, you can grab a quick bite at the **Jurassic Cafe**. This quick-service restaurant serves a range of delicious comfort food like ribs, pulled pork sandwiches, and dino-shaped chicken nuggets, perfect for a family meal or a fast snack.
2. **The Village Grill**
   - **Location**: Lower Lot, near **Transformers: The Ride 3D**.
   - **Cuisine**: Grilled burgers, hot dogs, and sides.
   - **Must-Try**: **Grilled chicken sandwiches, BBQ hot dogs**.
   - **Overview**: The **Village Grill** serves up tasty, simple grilled fare perfect for a quick break. Whether you're in the mood for a juicy chicken sandwich or a classic hot dog, it's an easy stop to refuel.

Sit-Down Meals:
1. **The Jurassic Park Restaurant**
   - **Location**: Lower Lot, adjacent to **Jurassic World: The Ride**.
   - **Cuisine**: Themed dining with American fare.
   - **Must-Try**: **BBQ chicken, bacon-wrapped meatloaf**, and **dino-size sides**.
   - **Overview**: Themed to the iconic Jurassic Park franchise, this sit-down restaurant is a fun and immersive experience where guests can enjoy hearty

meals in a unique atmosphere. From BBQ chicken to meatloaf, it's a great spot to relax after a thrilling ride through the park.

2. **Pink's Hot Dogs**
   o **Location**: Lower Lot, near **The Simpsons Ride**.
   o **Cuisine**: Famous hot dogs.
   o **Must-Try**: **Classic chili dog**, **Bacon chili cheese dog**.
   o **Overview**: **Pink's Hot Dogs** is a Hollywood institution, and their stand at Universal Studios Hollywood is the perfect spot for a delicious, quick sit-down meal. The hot dogs are packed with flavor, and you can add toppings like chili, cheese, or bacon for an extra treat.

Snacks Throughout the Park

No trip to Universal Studios Hollywood is complete without a few delicious snacks to enjoy while you explore the park. Here are some popular snack options to keep you going throughout the day:

1. **Giant Pretzels**: Available at various stands throughout the park, these soft, warm pretzels are a classic snack for any theme park goer. Try them with cheese or mustard for extra flavor.
2. **Popcorn**: Universal Studios Hollywood offers **buttery popcorn** available in various areas of the park, including specialty carts and shops. It's an easy-to-carry snack for those on the go.
3. **Ice Cream & Frozen Treats**: Whether it's a **Frozen Butterbeer** in the Wizarding World of Harry Potter or a classic scoop of **ice cream** from the park's various stands, there are plenty of options to cool down on hot days.
4. **Fruit Snacks & Granola Bars**: For a healthier option, you can find **fruit snacks** or **granola bars** available at snack

stands. These are great choices if you need a quick and energizing snack while you're exploring the park.

5. **Cotton Candy**: A fun and colorful treat, cotton candy is available at various snack carts. Choose from a variety of flavors and enjoy a sweet treat while strolling the park.

Dining Tips and Recommendations:

- **Make Reservations for Sit-Down Meals**: Popular sit-down restaurants like **Bubba Gump Shrimp Co.** and **The Three Broomsticks** can get busy, especially during peak times. Consider making **reservations** to ensure you get a seat at your desired time.

- **Mobile Ordering**: Many quick-service restaurants at Universal Studios Hollywood offer **mobile ordering** through the official app. This is a great way to avoid long lines and save time.

- **Dietary Restrictions**: If you have specific dietary needs, Universal Studios Hollywood offers a range of options, including **vegetarian**, **vegan**, and **gluten-free** items at several restaurants. Be sure to check menus ahead of time or ask restaurant staff for recommendations.

- **Stay Hydrated**: The California sun can get hot, especially during summer months, so be sure to stay hydrated. **Water refill stations** are available throughout the park, or you can buy bottled water from most food stands.

Universal Studios Hollywood offers a variety of dining experiences to suit every type of guest. Whether you're grabbing a quick bite between rides or sitting down for a full meal with the family, you'll find a wide range of food options across the park. From the themed meals in **Hogwarts** to the **Jurassic Park-inspired** dining spots, there's something for every taste and every pace. Plan your meals according to your schedule, and be sure to enjoy the diverse flavors and fun atmosphere that Universal Studios Hollywood has to offer!

Must-Try Themed Food at Universal Studios Hollywood: Butterbeer, Minion Treats, and More

When visiting **Universal Studios Hollywood**, the food is not just about eating—it's an experience! Themed food and beverages are a key part of the immersive atmosphere of the park, allowing you to indulge in the flavors of your favorite movies and franchises. From **Butterbeer** to **Minion treats**

1. Butterbeer: The Magic of the Wizarding World
- **Location**: The **Wizarding World of Harry Potter**
- **What It Is**: **Butterbeer** is a must-try drink for Harry Potter fans. It's a frothy, creamy beverage that captures the magical essence of the Wizarding World.
- **Flavors**: There are three main varieties of **Butterbeer**:
    - **Cold Butterbeer** (served with a frothy, sweet top)
    - **Frozen Butterbeer** (blended ice, perfect for a hot day)
    - **Hot Butterbeer** (ideal for cooler weather, with a comforting warmth)
- **Taste**: The drink has a rich, butterscotch flavor with a light, sweet, and creamy finish. It's both refreshing and indulgent, perfect for sipping while strolling through the Wizarding World.
- **Where to Find**: **The Three Broomsticks, The Butterbeer Cart** near the entrance to **Hogsmeade**, and **The Hog's Head Pub**.
- **Must-Try**: If you're new to Butterbeer, start with the **Frozen Butterbeer**—it's a fan favorite.

2. Minion Treats: Fun and Colorful Delights
- **Location**: **Despicable Me Minion Mayhem** area, Springfield

- **What It Is**: Inspired by the lovable, mischievous **Minions** from the **Despicable Me** movies, this section of the park offers a variety of cute and delicious themed snacks.
- **Must-Try Treats**:
  - **Minion Banana Cream Pie**: A nod to the Minions' obsession with bananas, this dessert is a fun and tasty combination of creamy banana pudding and pie crust.
  - **Minion Donut**: This adorable, yellow donut is topped with blue frosting and has a Minion face. It's sweet, fluffy, and a delightful snack for those with a sweet tooth.
  - **Minion Cupcakes**: Light vanilla or banana cupcakes with blue and yellow frosting, often adorned with Minion faces, these are perfect for a quick snack or dessert.
- **Where to Find**: **Minion Café**, the kiosks and stands in **Minion Land** (Springfield).
- **Must-Try**: If you're a fan of bananas, try the **Minion Banana Cream Pie**—it's a fun and delicious way to indulge in a treat inspired by the cheeky Minions.

3. Krusty Burger and Sideshow Bob's Favorite Treats
- **Location**: **Springfield**, next to **The Simpsons Ride**.
- **What It Is**: Universal's **Springfield** area brings the iconic animated world of **The Simpsons** to life. The food here mirrors the quirky, offbeat world of the show, with dishes inspired by **Krusty the Clown** and other Springfield characters.
- **Must-Try**:
  - **Krusty Burger**: A hearty, juicy burger named after the clown himself. The **Krusty Burger** is served with all the fixings and is often paired with fries or onion rings.

- o **Clogger Burger**: A massive burger for those with a big appetite, featuring multiple patties, cheese, bacon, and a special sauce.
  - o **Lard Lad Donuts**: **Lard Lad** is a famous character in Springfield, and his **giant donuts** are a fun and delicious treat. The oversized donut is perfect for sharing or indulging in all by yourself.
- **Where to Find**: **Krusty Burger, Lard Lad Donuts, The Frying Dutchman**.
- **Must-Try**: For a true **Simpsons** experience, the **Krusty Burger** is a must. It's a satisfying, classic American burger with all the elements fans of the show will love.

4. Jurassic Park-Themed Eats

- **Location**: **Jurassic World: The Ride** area, Lower Lot
- **What It Is**: If you're a fan of **Jurassic Park** and **Jurassic World**, you'll love the themed food offerings in this area, where dinosaurs rule.
- **Must-Try Treats**:
  - o **Raptor Ribs**: These are served as part of the **Jurassic Cafe**'s menu, inspired by the legendary carnivores from the park. Tender, smoky ribs served with sides like mashed potatoes and corn on the cob are perfect for fans of hearty meals.
  - o **Bacon-Wrapped Meatloaf**: An all-American classic with a Jurassic twist, the **bacon-wrapped meatloaf** is a filling and savory choice for those looking to enjoy a larger meal.

- **Where to Find**: **Jurassic Cafe**.
- **Must-Try**: The **Raptor Ribs** are a fan favorite—tender and flavorful with a great smoky finish.

5. Toadstool Café: Mushroom-Inspired Fare

- **Location**: **Super Nintendo World**
- **What It Is**: This charming café in **Super Nintendo World** combines quirky, mushroom-inspired design with delicious dishes.
- **Must-Try**:
    - **Power-Up Mushroom Soup**: A creamy soup served in a **Power-Up Mushroom** bowl (perfect for any Mario fan).
    - **Super Mushroom Burger**: A unique burger featuring mushrooms and cheese, served with crispy fries.
    - **Mario's Mystery Box Cake**: A fun and whimsical dessert that looks like a **mystery box** from the Mario games, and features a sweet, rich filling that's bound to please anyone with a sweet tooth.
- **Where to Find**: **Toadstool Café** in **Super Nintendo World**.
- **Must-Try**: The **Power-Up Mushroom Soup** offers a delicious and immersive experience that will leave you feeling like you're part of the Mario universe.

6. Giant Lard Lad Donut

- **Location**: **Springfield**
- **What It Is**: **Lard Lad Donuts** has been serving up these giant, fluffy, sugar-coated treats for years, and they're a must-try for anyone visiting the park. This donut is an iconic snack in **Springfield**, and it's bigger than your average donut.
- **Must-Try**: The **giant Lard Lad donut** is perfect for sharing or for treating yourself to a delicious, sugar-packed snack.
- **Where to Find**: **Lard Lad Donuts** in **Springfield**.
- **Must-Try**: You can't go wrong with the classic **giant Lard Lad donut**—it's a fun and iconic treat.

7. Hot Buttered Popcorn

- **Location**: Available throughout the park.
- **What It Is**: A classic theme park snack, **hot buttered popcorn** is a staple at Universal Studios Hollywood. It's freshly made and served warm with buttery goodness.
- **Where to Find**: Available at various carts and stands throughout the park.
- **Must-Try**: Perfect for snacking on while you explore or wait for a ride. It's a simple yet satisfying treat for all ages.

8. Frozen Banana at the Banana Stand

- **Location**: **Springfield**.
- **What It Is**: A fun and quirky treat inspired by the **Frozen Banana Stand** from the **Arrested Development** series.
- **Must-Try**: A **Frozen Banana** dipped in chocolate and sprinkles.
- **Where to Find**: **Frozen Banana Stand** in **Springfield**.
- **Must-Try**: A **Frozen Banana** is both refreshing and indulgent, perfect for a quick treat on a warm day.

From the magical flavors of **Butterbeer** to the playful treats inspired by **The Simpsons** and **Super Mario**, Universal Studios Hollywood offers an exciting array of themed food that enhances your park experience. Be sure to indulge in these fun, flavorful treats to make your visit even more memorable. Whether you're looking for something sweet, savory, or completely whimsical, there's a themed food item for every type of fan at the park.

Vegetarian, Vegan, and Gluten-Free Options at Universal Studios Hollywood

Universal Studios Hollywood offers a variety of options for guests with dietary restrictions or preferences, ensuring that everyone can enjoy the park's food offerings. Whether you're vegetarian, vegan, or gluten-free, the park has plenty of delicious meals to suit your needs.

Here's a detailed guide to navigating the food scene for each dietary preference:

Vegetarian Options

1. Three Broomsticks (Wizarding World of Harry Potter)
- **Vegetarian Shepherd's Pie**: A savory pie filled with vegetables, topped with mashed potatoes. It's a hearty, meatless alternative for guests seeking a filling meal.
- **Cauldron-Cooked Vegetable Soup**: A rich and flavorful soup made with seasonal vegetables. It's served with bread, making it a comforting choice for vegetarians.
- **Pumpkin Juice**: A sweet and spicy beverage that's a hit among vegetarians and is perfect when paired with any meal.

2. Universal CityWalk – Voodoo Doughnut
- **Vegan Doughnuts**: Voodoo Doughnut offers several vegan doughnut options, including the **Maple Bacon Bar** and the **Vegan Oreo Doughnut**, both made with plant-based ingredients and perfect for those avoiding dairy or eggs.

3. Jurassic Café (Lower Lot)
- **Vegetarian Tacos**: Soft tortillas filled with grilled vegetables, beans, and rice, offering a fresh and flavorful option.
- **Vegetarian Burger**: A hearty veggie patty topped with all the traditional burger fixings. Available for those who prefer plant-based meals.
- **Fruit and Nut Salads**: Light and refreshing salads with mixed greens, nuts, and fruits. Add a dressing of your choice for an extra kick.

4. Krusty Burger (Springfield)
- **Veggie Burger**: A delicious meatless burger made from plant-based ingredients, served with all the traditional fixings like lettuce, tomato, pickles, and sauce.

- **Krusty's Side Salad**: A simple side salad with mixed greens, cucumber, and tomato—perfect for a light snack or meal accompaniment.

5. Minion Café (Minion Land)

- **Vegetarian Fried Rice**: A vibrant, veggie-packed rice dish with peas, carrots, and soy sauce—served as a side or main dish.
- **Cauliflower Tacos**: Crispy cauliflower served in soft tortillas with fresh toppings, a popular vegetarian choice that's both satisfying and flavorful.

Vegan Options

1. Toadstool Café (Super Nintendo World)

- **Vegan Mushroom Soup**: A creamy, hearty soup made with mushrooms and plant-based ingredients, served in a **Power-Up Mushroom** bowl. It's a warming, filling option for vegan guests.
- **Vegan Super Mushroom Burger**: A plant-based burger made with a vegan patty, served with lettuce, tomato, and other fresh veggies.
- **Vegan Cookie**: A sweet and chewy dessert option for those following a plant-based diet.

2. Springfield – The Frying Dutchman

- **Vegan Fish-less Filet Sandwich**: A plant-based version of the iconic fried fish sandwich. The crispy, vegan "fish" is battered and served on a bun with pickles and a tangy sauce.
- **Vegan French Fries**: Golden and crispy, these fries are perfect for pairing with any vegan dish. They're fried in a separate oil to avoid cross-contamination.
- **Vegan Beetroot Burger**: A savory burger made from beetroot and other plant-based ingredients. It's served with lettuce, tomato, and your choice of sauce.

3. Universal CityWalk – Blaze Pizza

- **Vegan Pizza**: Blaze offers customizable pizzas with a variety of plant-based toppings, vegan cheese, and gluten-free crust options. Choose from ingredients like artichokes, mushrooms, and roasted vegetables for a fulfilling meal.
- **Vegan Salad**: A hearty salad filled with fresh vegetables, nuts, and seeds, drizzled with a light vinaigrette dressing.

4. Minion Café (Minion Land)

- **Vegan Mac and Cheese**: A creamy, plant-based mac and cheese made with cashew cheese, offering a rich, cheesy flavor without any dairy.
- **Vegan Nachos**: Crispy tortilla chips piled high with vegan cheese, guacamole, salsa, and jalapeños—a fun and shareable snack for any vegan.

Gluten-Free Options

1. The Wizarding World of Harry Potter

- **Gluten-Free Fish and Chips (The Three Broomsticks)**: Enjoy the classic fish and chips meal made with gluten-free batter, ensuring those with gluten sensitivities can enjoy this English favorite.
- **Gluten-Free Shepherd's Pie**: A hearty vegetable-based pie topped with mashed potatoes—perfect for those avoiding gluten.
- **Gluten-Free Butterbeer**: All three versions of **Butterbeer** (cold, frozen, and hot) are naturally gluten-free, so you can enjoy this magical treat worry-free.

2. Jurassic Café (Lower Lot)

- **Gluten-Free Grilled Chicken Salad**: A light, refreshing salad topped with grilled chicken breast and served with a gluten-free dressing.
- **Gluten-Free Tacos**: Soft corn tortillas filled with seasoned grilled chicken or vegetables, providing a safe, gluten-free option.

3. Krusty Burger (Springfield)

- **Gluten-Free Veggie Burger**: A gluten-free bun option is available for the **Veggie Burger**, offering a delicious and safe meal for those avoiding gluten.
- **Gluten-Free French Fries**: The crispy fries here are gluten-free, making them a perfect accompaniment to any meal.

4. Minion Café (Minion Land)

- **Gluten-Free Cauliflower Tacos**: Crispy, flavorful cauliflower served in soft, gluten-free tortillas, creating a satisfying and safe meal.
- **Gluten-Free Pasta**: A pasta option made with gluten-free noodles, topped with a hearty marinara sauce and vegetables.

5. Universal CityWalk – P.F. Chang's

- **Gluten-Free Asian Lettuce Wraps**: A classic starter made with marinated chicken, vegetables, and gluten-free soy sauce, served in crispy lettuce cups.
- **Gluten-Free Kung Pao Chicken**: A flavorful stir-fry dish made with chicken, peanuts, and gluten-free sauce—perfect for gluten-free diners.

Additional Tips for Dietary Restrictions

- **Allergen-Free Menu**: Many locations within the park provide allergen-free menus upon request. Be sure to ask the staff for a special menu if you have concerns about food allergies.
- **Gluten-Free and Vegan Substitutes**: Most counter-service restaurants and cafes are happy to accommodate gluten-free or

vegan substitutions. Don't hesitate to ask for plant-based or gluten-free alternatives to bread, buns, or sauces.

Universal Studios Hollywood strives to offer a variety of vegetarian, vegan, and gluten-free options to accommodate all dietary needs, ensuring every guest has a delightful experience. Whether you're enjoying a magical **Butterbeer** or savoring a delicious **vegan taco**, you'll find plenty of tasty and satisfying options that keep your dietary preferences in mind while allowing you to fully immerse yourself in the theme park experience.

CHAPTER 7

Shopping and Souvenirs at Universal Studios Hollywood: A Shopper's Paradise

Universal Studios Hollywood isn't just a theme park—it's also a treasure trove for unique and exclusive souvenirs that will let you take home a piece of the magic. From **Harry Potter wands** to **Minion plushies**, the park offers an array of themed merchandise that makes for the perfect keepsake or gift. Whether you're looking for something iconic or seeking an exclusive collectible, this guide has all the details you need to navigate Universal Studios Hollywood's shopping scene.

1. Top Souvenir Shops: From Harry Potter Wands to Minion Plushies

The Wizarding World of Harry Potter

- **Ollivanders Wand Shop**: Step into **Ollivanders** in **Hogsmeade** and feel the magic as you browse through a selection of hand-crafted wands. Whether you're a Gryffindor, Slytherin, Ravenclaw, or Hufflepuff, there's a wand waiting for you. The shop is known for offering a wide variety of wands, from the famous **Harry Potter wand** to those of beloved characters like **Hermione Granger** and **Dumbledore**. You can also find special wands that interact with various spots around the Wizarding World.
    - o **Must-Have: Interactive Wands**—These wands allow you to cast spells around Hogsmeade and Diagon Alley, making your visit even more immersive.
- **Honeydukes**: This beloved sweet shop in the heart of **Hogsmeade** offers a wide variety of candy and treats straight

from the Harry Potter universe, including **Bertie Bott's Every Flavor Beans**, **Chocolate Frogs**, and **Pumpkin Pasties**. You'll also find a range of adorable Hogwarts-themed mugs, hats, and clothing items.

- o **Must-Have**: **Chocolate Frogs** and **Bertie Bott's Every Flavor Beans**—both iconic treats from the Harry Potter books and films.

Minion Land (Springfield)

- **Minion Mart**: Themed after the adorable Minions from **Despicable Me**, **Minion Mart** offers everything from plush toys to apparel and accessories. You'll find a wide selection of Minion-themed clothing, including T-shirts, hats, socks, and even backpacks. The shelves are filled with quirky collectibles, from **Minion plush toys** to **Minion mugs**.
  - o **Must-Have**: A **Minion Plushie**—these cute and cuddly characters are perfect for any fan, big or small.

Super Nintendo World

- **1-UP Factory**: For all things **Super Mario**, this store offers a treasure trove of **Nintendo-themed merchandise**. You can pick up action figures, T-shirts, hats, and plush toys inspired by iconic characters like **Mario**, **Luigi**, and **Princess Peach**. Don't miss the **Mario Kart**-themed items, which are exclusive to Universal Studios Hollywood.
  - o **Must-Have**: A **Power-Up Band**—this wearable band enhances your experience in Super Nintendo World and can be used to interact with various activities and challenges in the park.
- **Toadstool Café Gift Shop**: This smaller gift shop inside **Toadstool Café** offers exclusive **Super Nintendo World** merchandise, including quirky mushroom-inspired items and exclusive limited-edition pins.

o **Must-Have**: **Super Mushroom Plushie**—A cute and colorful plush that fans of Mario will love.

Jurassic Park Area

- **Jurassic Outfitters**: This store offers a wide array of **Jurassic Park** and **Jurassic World** merchandise, from t-shirts and hats to toys and collectibles. You can also find realistic dinosaur-themed items such as **Raptor figurines, Jurassic Park-themed jewelry**, and **Jurassic World apparel**.
  o **Must-Have**: A **T-Rex Plushie**—bring home your very own dino friend with this adorable plush.

2. Exclusive Merchandise

Universal Studios Hollywood is home to many **exclusive collectibles** and limited-edition items that can't be found anywhere else. Whether you're an avid collector or just looking for something unique, here are some of the exclusive merchandise offerings you won't want to miss:

- **Limited-Edition Pins**: The park offers a wide selection of collectible pins featuring iconic rides, attractions, characters, and even special event pins. These pins are perfect for pin collectors or as a memento from your trip.
  o **Where to Find**: Available at most gift shops, including **Ollivanders, Minion Mart**, and **1-UP Factory**.
  o **Must-Have**: Look out for **limited-edition event pins** celebrating special occasions or anniversaries at the park.
- **Jurassic World Collectibles**: For fans of the **Jurassic World** franchise, exclusive **Jurassic Park T-shirts, dinosaur replicas**, and **life-sized dino models** are available. These items are perfect for displaying in your home or adding to your collection.
  o **Where to Find**: **Jurassic Outfitters** and various stands around the park.

- **Exclusive Movie-Themed Apparel**: From **The Simpsons** to **Fast & Furious**, the park carries exclusive **movie-themed clothing** not available outside the park. Look for **Fast & Furious jackets**, **Simpsons hoodies**, and **Harry Potter scarves**.
  - ○ **Where to Find**: Shops in **Springfield**, **Hogsmeade**, and **Super Nintendo World**.

3. Shopping Tips to Save Money

While Universal Studios Hollywood is known for its high-quality merchandise, there are ways to save money while shopping for souvenirs. Here are some tips to help you get the most bang for your buck:

- **Buy Souvenirs Early in the Day**: Sometimes, certain items like plush toys or limited-edition collectibles can sell out quickly. Shopping early in the day gives you the best chance to snag your favorite items before they're gone.
- **Look for Package Deals**: Certain stores and attractions offer **bundle deals** for merchandise. For example, you can often buy a **wand and robe combo** at a discounted price in **Ollivanders**. Similarly, **Minion plushies** are often available in a bundle deal that includes a t-shirt or accessory at a reduced price.
- **Check Out the Universal Studios Hollywood Website**: Sometimes, **exclusive online sales** or discounts are available before you even arrive at the park. Check out the website for special offers on items like **T-shirts** or **park-specific merchandise**.
- **Buy Merchandise Online After Your Visit**: If you didn't have time to shop during your visit, many of the park's popular items are available for purchase online through the Universal Studios Hollywood online store. You may even find discounts or promotions available for online purchases.

- **Consider an Annual Pass**: If you're a frequent visitor to the park, an **Annual Pass** often includes discounts on merchandise, food, and even special events. Make sure to inquire about the discount options when purchasing an Annual Pass.

4. Must-Have Souvenirs

- **Interactive Wands** (from **Ollivanders**)—These wands are a fan favorite and add an extra layer of magic to your visit to the **Wizarding World of Harry Potter**.
- **Minion Plushies** (from **Minion Mart**)—A must for any Minion fan, these cuddly toys are a perfect reminder of your time in the park.
- **Power-Up Band** (from **Super Nintendo World**)—A functional souvenir that enhances your experience and unlocks interactive activities in the **Super Nintendo World**.
- **Jurassic Park T-Rex Model** (from **Jurassic Outfitters**)—A highly detailed, collectible model for fans of the **Jurassic Park** franchise.
- **Simpsons T-Shirt** (from **Springfield**)—Celebrate your time in **Springfield** with iconic shirts featuring the Simpson family or catchy quotes.

Shopping at **Universal Studios Hollywood** is an experience in itself. With a wide range of themed souvenirs, exclusive merchandise, and plenty of opportunities to save money, there's something for everyone to take home as a reminder of their adventure. Whether you're a Harry Potter fan, a lover of Minions, or a collector of all things Jurassic, the park's shops offer an unforgettable selection of goods that are perfect for fans of all ages.

COLLECTIBLES AT UNIVERSAL STUDIOS

CHAPTER 8

Tips for Families Visiting Universal Studios Hollywood

Rides and Activities for All Ages

Universal Studios Hollywood is a fantastic destination for families, offering an exciting mix of attractions, rides, and live shows that cater to a wide range of ages and interests. Whether you have toddlers, tweens, or teens, there's something for everyone in the family to enjoy. This guide will help you navigate the park with children in tow, highlighting kid-friendly rides, activities, and essential tips to make your visit smooth and enjoyable for all ages.

1. Kid-Friendly Rides and Attractions

A. Upper Lot Attractions:

- **The Wizarding World of Harry Potter**
  - **Flight of the Hippogriff**: This is a gentle, family-friendly roller coaster that's perfect for young children. It's themed around the magical world of Harry Potter, offering a chance to fly past Hagrid's hut and around the majestic **Hogwarts Castle**. The ride is not too intense, making it a great option for younger guests.
  - **Must-Do for Kids**: **Butterbeer**—A non-alcoholic, frothy drink available in both frozen and cold varieties. It's a sweet treat that young Potterheads will love.
- **Despicable Me: Minion Mayhem**:
  - This 3D motion simulator ride immerses you in the world of **Gru** and his mischievous Minions. It's

suitable for children of all ages and features fun, lighthearted action that's more comical than scary.

- o **Must-Do for Kids**: The **Minion Plushies** and other Minion-themed merchandise available in **Minion Mart**. These soft toys are perfect for children to snuggle and bring home.

- **The Simpsons Ride**:
  - o This is another 3D motion simulator, but it's ideal for slightly older children or those who enjoy wacky, cartoon-style humor. The ride takes you on a wild adventure through **Springfield**, home of the Simpsons.
  - o **Tip for Families**: This ride might be a little intense for younger children, so check the ride's height requirement and prepare for some dizzying twists and turns.

- **Secret Life of Pets: Off the Leash**:
  - o This newer attraction is an indoor dark ride that takes families through the adventures of **Max** and his animal friends. It's a delightful, interactive ride for younger guests, featuring vibrant characters and lots of humor.
  - o **Perfect for**: Families with toddlers and young kids, as it's gentle and full of cute and engaging animal characters.

B. Lower Lot Attractions:

- **Jurassic World: The Ride**:
  - o While this ride features some thrilling elements, including a massive drop at the end, it's still great for families with older children or those who enjoy a bit of excitement. It's a water ride with lifelike animatronic dinosaurs, including the iconic **T-Rex**.
  - o **Tip for Families**: Younger kids might get spooked by the roar of the dinosaurs, but it's not overly scary for

children who enjoy a little adventure. Be prepared to get a little wet!

- **Transformers: The Ride 3D**:
  - This high-tech, motion-simulated ride is an exciting and intense 3D adventure. It's ideal for families with older children and teens who love action-packed experiences.
  - **Tip for Families**: Due to the intense motion and quick movements, this ride is recommended for kids who are used to thrilling rides and not for younger children who may be sensitive to fast-paced experiences.

- **Revenge of the Mummy: The Ride**:
  - This indoor roller coaster offers a mix of thrills and dark, creepy elements. While it's thrilling, it's on the milder side compared to some other roller coasters, making it suitable for kids who enjoy a bit of excitement.
  - **Perfect for**: Families with kids who are ready for their first roller coaster experience.

2. Live Shows and Entertainment

Universal Studios Hollywood offers a range of live shows and interactive experiences, which are ideal for families looking to take a break from the rides. These shows offer plenty of entertainment for all ages and give everyone a chance to relax and enjoy something new.

- **WaterWorld: A Live Sea War Spectacular**:
  - This high-energy stunt show is full of explosions, thrilling action sequences, and daring feats of acrobatics. It's exciting but not overwhelming for kids, making it a must-see for families. Be prepared to sit in the **"soak zone"** if you want to get splashed!

- o **Tip for Families**: Arrive early to get a good spot, especially if you're sitting in the **soak zone**, as these seats are closest to the action.
- **The Special Effects Show**:
  - o A behind-the-scenes look at the magic of film-making, this interactive show demonstrates how special effects, explosions, and stunts are created in Hollywood. It's educational yet entertaining, perfect for curious kids who are interested in the movie-making process.
  - o **Great for**: Kids who are into movies or aspiring filmmakers. It's engaging for all ages and offers a fascinating look into the world of Hollywood.
- **Character Meet-and-Greets**:
  - o A huge highlight for young fans is meeting their favorite characters. Universal Studios Hollywood offers the chance to meet iconic characters like **Minions**, **Harry Potter** characters, and even **Transformers**. Kids will love getting autographs and taking photos with these larger-than-life figures.
  - o **Tip for Families**: Check the daily schedule for character meet-and-greet times so you can plan ahead and avoid long waits.

3. Parent Tips: Making Your Visit Easier
A. Use the Universal Studios App:
- Download the **Universal Studios Hollywood app** before your visit. It provides real-time updates on wait times for attractions, show schedules, and location maps. It's a great way to plan your day and minimize time spent in long lines.

B. Take Advantage of Child Swap:
- For families with young kids who may not meet height requirements for certain rides, Universal Studios offers a **Child Swap** program. One parent can ride while the other

stays with the child, and then you can swap without waiting in line again.

C. Consider a Stroller Rental:

- Universal Studios Hollywood offers stroller rentals at the park entrance. If you have young children who may tire easily, renting a stroller is a great way to keep them comfortable while navigating the park. Be sure to reserve your stroller early, especially during busy times.

D. Pack Snacks and Water:

- While there are plenty of food options within the park, it's always a good idea to bring some snacks for your kids to keep them energized throughout the day. There are also water refill stations around the park, so be sure to stay hydrated.

E. Plan for Naptime:

- If you have younger children who still nap, plan to take breaks in quieter areas of the park. The **Studio Tour** provides a chance for kids to relax while still experiencing the magic of Universal Studios Hollywood.

4. Dining Tips for Families

Universal Studios Hollywood offers a variety of dining options, with some perfect for families with kids:

- **Fast Food & Quick Service**: Many restaurants around the park offer kid-friendly meals, such as **chicken tenders**, **mac and cheese**, **burgers**, and **pizza**. Consider stopping at **Minion Café**, **Krusty Burger**, or **Jurassic Café** for a quick bite.
- **Dining for Special Occasions**: For a sit-down experience, try **The Three Broomsticks** (in the Wizarding World of Harry Potter) or **Mel's Diner** in **Hollywood**, offering both kid-friendly menus and fun theming.

- **Kids' Menus**: Most restaurants offer specialized kids' meals with smaller portions and lower prices, such as **mini burgers**, **hot dogs**, and **fruit cups**.

5. Conclusion: A Family-Friendly Adventure

Universal Studios Hollywood is a magical destination for families, offering an exciting blend of attractions, shows, and dining options for kids of all ages. From gentle rides like **Flight of the Hippogriff** to action-packed experiences like **Jurassic World: The Ride**, there's something for everyone. By planning ahead and using the helpful tips in this guide, your family can make the most out of your visit, creating memories that will last a lifetime.

Baby Care Centers and Kid-Friendly Amenities at Universal Studios Hollywood

Universal Studios Hollywood is designed to be a family-friendly destination, offering a variety of amenities that cater to families with young children. Whether you need to take a break, change a diaper, or find a quiet spot to feed your little one, the park offers several resources to help manage your day smoothly. Below is everything you need to know about **baby care centers**, **kid-friendly amenities**, and **managing strollers and baby gear** to make your visit as stress-free as possible.

1. Baby Care Centers

Universal Studios Hollywood has a **Baby Care Center** to assist parents with the needs of their young children, from diaper changes to feeding breaks. This center is a must-know for families visiting the park.

Location:

- The **Baby Care Center** is located in the **Upper Lot**, near the **Studio Tour** entrance. It is centrally located and easily accessible.

Facilities and Features:

- **Private Nursing Rooms**: The Baby Care Center offers comfortable, quiet rooms for nursing mothers, providing a private space to feed your baby.
- **Changing Tables**: Clean, spacious changing tables are available for diaper changes. The area is equipped with all the essentials for a quick and easy diaper change.
- **Bottle Warmers**: For parents who are bottle-feeding, the Baby Care Center has bottle warmers to heat up your baby's milk or formula.
- **High Chairs**: If you need to feed your baby solid food, high chairs are available for your convenience.
- **Parenting Supplies**: The Baby Care Center also offers a small selection of **diapers**, **wipes**, **baby food**, and other essentials for purchase if you find you've forgotten something at home.
- **Seating Areas**: There are comfortable seating areas where parents can sit and relax while attending to their babies.
- **Microwave**: A microwave is available if you need to heat up baby food or snacks.

Hours of Operation:

- The **Baby Care Center** generally follows park hours, but it's a good idea to check with park staff on the day of your visit for any changes to operating hours.

2. Kid-Friendly Amenities and Services

Universal Studios Hollywood offers several other kid-friendly amenities throughout the park to ensure families with young children have an enjoyable and convenient experience.

Stroller Rentals:

- **Location**: Stroller rentals are available near the **park entrance**.

- **Standard Strollers**: Universal offers standard single and double strollers for rent. They are perfect for young children who might tire easily from walking around the park.
- **Cost**: Rental prices typically range from **$15 to $35** for a single stroller and a little more for a double stroller. Rates are subject to change, so be sure to check the most current prices at the rental counter.
- **Tip**: Stroller rentals are **first-come, first-served**, so it's a good idea to rent one early, especially on busy days.

Stroller Parking:
- Universal Studios Hollywood offers designated **stroller parking areas** near the entrance of each major attraction. This is a great option if you want to leave your stroller behind while enjoying certain rides or shows.
- **Tip**: Don't forget to label your stroller with your name or a unique identifier to avoid mix-ups.

Baby-Change Stations:
- **Locations**: In addition to the Baby Care Center, there are **baby-change stations** located throughout the park, including in the **restrooms** in both the Upper and Lower Lots.
- **Facilities**: These stations include clean, spacious tables, and are equipped with all the essentials to help you manage diaper changes while out and about in the park.

Kid-Friendly Rides with No Height Requirements:
- Universal Studios Hollywood offers several rides and attractions with no height restrictions, making them perfect for families with toddlers or babies:
  - **Despicable Me: Minion Mayhem**: A 3D motion-simulator ride that's suitable for younger kids.
  - **The Wizarding World of Harry Potter**: Rides like **Flight of the Hippogriff** and the interactive wand experience are fun for families with young kids.

- The Secret Life of Pets: Off the Leash: A gentle ride featuring beloved characters from the **Secret Life of Pets** movies.

Family Restrooms:

- Family restrooms are available throughout the park, offering spacious and private areas for parents and children to use the facilities together. They are ideal for those with toddlers or families who need extra space.

3. Managing Strollers and Baby Gear

Taking care of strollers and baby gear is important when navigating the park, especially on busy days. Here are some key tips for managing your stroller and baby gear while at Universal Studios Hollywood:

A. Renting a Stroller vs. Bringing Your Own

- **Renting a Stroller**: Renting a stroller at the park is convenient if you prefer not to bring your own. Rental strollers are lightweight and easy to maneuver, but they can be somewhat basic.
    - **Advantages**: Saves you the hassle of transporting your own stroller, and it's especially handy if you're flying in for your trip.
    - **Disadvantages**: Limited choice of stroller styles or sizes. You may also find it harder to store extra baby gear like diaper bags in rented strollers.
- **Bringing Your Own Stroller**: If you prefer your own stroller, bringing it is a good option. Make sure your stroller is easy to fold and store, as many rides and attractions require strollers to be parked or folded up.
    - **Advantages**: You'll be familiar with your own stroller, and it can carry extra items like diaper bags or baby food. Plus, you may have more storage options.
    - **Disadvantages**: Navigating through crowds can be a bit more challenging, especially during peak times.

You'll also need to be mindful of where to park your stroller while riding attractions.

B. Baby Gear Storage

- **Lockers**: Universal Studios Hollywood provides **lockers** for rent throughout the park. If you have extra baby gear that you don't need at all times, renting a locker for storage is a good option. Lockers are available in various sizes, so you can store items like strollers, diaper bags, or extra clothes.
  - o **Tip**: Lockers are available for a **fee**, typically ranging from **$10 to $25** depending on the size and location.

C. Baby Food and Snacks

- **Feeding Options**: There are plenty of places to grab snacks for your kids, but if your baby needs special foods or formula, consider bringing your own. The **Baby Care Center** provides **bottle warmers** and microwaves for parents to use, but some items may be more easily brought from home.
- **Baby Food in the Park**: Most of the **quick-service restaurants** at Universal Studios offer **kid-friendly meals** like chicken tenders, macaroni and cheese, or pizza. However, **healthy baby food** options like jars or pouches may need to be brought with you.
- **Snack Tip**: Bring along some **snack bars** or **fruit pouches** to keep your baby or toddler happy and energized throughout the day.

D. Keeping Your Baby Comfortable

- **Sunscreen**: Apply sunscreen on your baby before heading out into the sun, and bring extra sunscreen with you for reapplication throughout the day. Universal Studios Hollywood offers **baby-safe sunscreen** in their gift shops, but it's better to bring your own.
- **Hats & Sunglasses**: To protect your little one from the sun, make sure they wear a **hat** and **sunglasses** while exploring the park.

- **Cooling Towels**: If you're visiting on a hot day, cooling towels are a great way to keep babies comfortable, especially in areas where there's little shade. You can find them at many shops or bring your own.

4. Stress-Free Park Experience with Babies and Young Kids
Universal Studios Hollywood is dedicated to making your visit with young children as enjoyable as possible. With amenities like the **Baby Care Center**, **stroller rentals**, and **kid-friendly attractions**, the park ensures that parents can focus on fun while easily managing baby needs. By utilizing these family-friendly amenities and following the tips for managing strollers and baby gear, you'll have a smoother experience and make the most of your family day at the park.

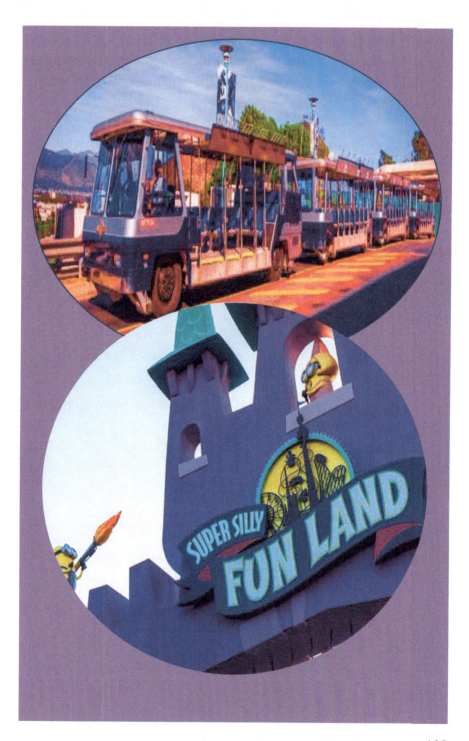

CHAPTER 9

Seasonal Events at Universal Studios Hollywood

Universal Studios Hollywood is known for its immersive, high-energy events that change throughout the year, bringing something special for guests to enjoy during different seasons. From spine-chilling horror nights to festive Lunar New Year celebrations, here's a detailed guide to some of the most popular seasonal events you can experience at the park.

1. Halloween Horror Nights

Halloween Horror Nights is one of Universal Studios Hollywood's most anticipated annual events, attracting fans of horror and thrill-seekers alike. Held in the fall, usually starting in mid-September and running through October, this event transforms the park into a fright-fest filled with terrifying haunted houses, scare zones, and live entertainment that will send shivers down your spine.

Dates and Timing:

- **When**: Halloween Horror Nights typically runs from **mid-September to the end of October**. It takes place in the evening, with the event usually starting around **7:00 PM** and running until midnight or later, depending on the night.

Tip: Be sure to check the official Universal Studios Hollywood website for specific event dates as the schedule can vary each year.

Event Highlights:

- **Haunted Houses**: These chilling attractions are the main draw of Halloween Horror Nights. Each year, Universal Studios Hollywood teams up with some of the scariest franchises in the horror world, including **The Walking Dead**, **Stranger Things**, **The Exorcist**, and more. Expect to walk through intricately designed haunted houses that are filled with creepy creatures, jump scares, and intense special effects.

- **Scare Zones**: Throughout the park, scare actors roam the streets, creating a spine-tingling atmosphere. These scare zones are designed to immerse you in terrifying settings where you may encounter creatures from popular horror films or original monsters crafted just for the event.

Tip: These zones can be pretty intense, so if you're bringing younger children or those who get scared easily, you might want to avoid certain areas.

- **Live Entertainment**: Halloween Horror Nights also features live shows with a spooky theme. These performances are often high-energy, mixing horror with theatrical elements, providing a break from the scares while still keeping the eerie vibe alive.

Example: "**The Jabbawockeez**" is a popular dance crew that often performs during Halloween Horror Nights, blending music and dance with a creepy twist.

- **Food and Drinks**: Themed food and drink options are available throughout the park during Halloween Horror

Nights. Expect to find seasonal treats like **pumpkin-flavored snacks**, **blood-red drinks**, and themed cocktails designed to fit the spooky atmosphere.

Tips for Halloween Horror Nights:

- **Arrive Early**: Halloween Horror Nights tends to get very crowded, especially as the night goes on. Arriving early gives you a better chance of enjoying more attractions before the crowds build up.
- **Stay Hydrated**: While you may be in for some scary fun, don't forget to stay hydrated, especially if you're running from haunted house to haunted house in the California heat.
- **Upgrade to VIP**: Consider purchasing a **VIP Experience** for access to **express entry** to the haunted houses, front-of-line privileges, and exclusive tours. This option makes the experience a lot less stressful during peak times.
- **Age Consideration**: This event is not recommended for young children. It can be very intense and may not be suitable for those under the age of 13, especially with the haunted houses and scare zones.

2. Lunar New Year Celebrations

Overview:

Universal Studios Hollywood celebrates Lunar New Year each year with vibrant cultural performances, special food, themed merchandise, and family-friendly activities. The event typically takes place in **January or February**, depending on the timing of the Lunar New Year, and it celebrates the traditions and customs of East and Southeast Asia.

Dates and Timing:

- **When**: Lunar New Year celebrations occur during the **Lunar New Year season**, which can vary, but it's typically held between **January and February**.
- **Tip**: Check the calendar for specific dates each year to make sure you're visiting during the celebration.

Event Highlights:

- **Cultural Performances**: Universal Studios Hollywood features vibrant **cultural performances** including **traditional Chinese lion dances**, **Korean drumming**, and **Taiwanese dance troupes**. These performances take place throughout the park and are perfect for getting into the festive spirit.
- **Mulan's Chinese New Year Procession**: A special show featuring the beloved Disney character **Mulan** and her friends. The colorful parade includes dancers, musicians, and characters celebrating the Lunar New Year with an energetic and beautiful procession.
- **Themed Decorations**: The park is beautifully decorated to mark the occasion, with intricate **red lanterns, golden dragons**, and other traditional Lunar New Year symbols. The festive decorations help set the mood, and it's a great opportunity for pictures!
- **Special Food and Treats**: As part of the celebration, Universal Studios Hollywood offers exclusive **Lunar New Year-themed**

food and snacks. From **dumplings** and **bao buns** to **sweet rice cakes** and **matcha-flavored desserts**, these treats provide guests with a taste of traditional Lunar New Year flavors.

Tip: Look for food stalls and carts in the **Upper Lot** and **Lower Lot** where these special offerings are sold. Some seasonal items are unique each year, so don't miss out!

- **Exclusive Merchandise**: If you're looking for souvenirs to remember the event, you'll find exclusive **Lunar New Year-themed merchandise** including shirts, plush toys, and special collectibles. Universal often collaborates with Disney to offer **exclusive Mulan and other Disney character-themed Lunar New Year items**.

- **Character Meet-and-Greets**: During Lunar New Year, you'll have the chance to meet some beloved Disney characters in festive attire. This often includes characters like **Mulan**, **Pooh Bear**, **Tigger**, and **other Disney friends** who are dressed in their New Year's best and ready for photos.

Tips for Lunar New Year Celebrations:

- **Get There Early**: Like most Universal seasonal events, the Lunar New Year festivities can get busy, so arriving early ensures you can enjoy the special performances and get front-row views of parades or shows.

- **Dress in Layers**: Since the event happens during the cooler months, dress in layers to stay comfortable during the day and evening when temperatures can drop.

- **Try the Food**: Don't miss out on trying the traditional treats offered for the Lunar New Year, such as **Chinese-style dumplings**, **hot pot**, and the **Sesame Seed Balls** for dessert.
- **Plan for Photos**: The decorations and characters are picture-perfect for families and anyone wanting to capture memories. Be sure to have your camera or smartphone ready!

Whether you're into spine-tingling thrills or cultural celebrations, Universal Studios Hollywood's seasonal events like **Halloween Horror Nights** and **Lunar New Year Celebrations** offer something for everyone. Halloween Horror Nights is perfect for those seeking scares and thrills, while Lunar New Year brings a festive, family-friendly atmosphere with cultural performances, food, and fun. Make sure to plan ahead, as these events are highly popular, and enjoy the magic that Universal Studios Hollywood brings to these seasonal festivities!

Grinchmas and Winter Wonderland at Universal Studios Hollywood (2025)
Universal Studios Hollywood offers an enchanting winter experience with its **Grinchmas** celebration and **Winter Wonderland**, creating a festive atmosphere for visitors of all ages. These seasonal events, along with other limited-time experiences, add an extra layer of magic to the park, making it a must-visit destination during the holiday season.

1. Grinchmas

Grinchmas is Universal Studios Hollywood's beloved holiday event that brings to life the world of Dr. Seuss's **How the Grinch Stole Christmas**. This festive celebration is perfect for families, offering everything from themed shows to a towering Christmas tree, all set within the whimsical, snow-dusted world of Whoville.

Event Dates:
- **When**: Grinchmas typically runs from **late November through early January**, coinciding with the holiday season.

Tip: Check the Universal Studios Hollywood website for specific dates and operating hours as they can vary depending on the year.

Event Highlights:
- **The Grinchmas Who-ville**: Visitors can step into the heart of Whoville, where the **Grinch** and his friends come to life. With festive decorations, Whoville-style homes, and cheerful characters, you'll feel like you've entered the pages of Dr. Seuss's classic story.
  - **Snowfall in Whoville**: The highlight of the Grinchmas

experience is the **snowfall** that takes place in Whoville. Watch as snow gently falls around you, adding to the magical winter wonderland atmosphere.

- **Grinchmas Tree Lighting Ceremony**: The grand centerpiece of Grinchmas is the stunning **Grinchmas Tree** in the heart of Whoville. Each night, the tree is lit up in a dazzling ceremony, with the Grinch himself making an appearance for a memorable photo op.
  - o **Tip**: Arrive early to secure a good spot for the tree lighting ceremony, as it's a popular event during the holiday season.

- **Meet-and-Greets with the Grinch**: One of the biggest draws of Grinchmas is the chance to meet the **Grinch** himself. He'll be available for photos, and you may even catch him being his mischievous self, interacting with visitors.

Tip: The Grinch often poses for fun photos, so be ready for some silly moments with this holiday classic villain.

- **Live Holiday Shows**: Enjoy live musical performances, including a **Whoville Holiday Show** where Whos from the classic story sing and dance to get everyone in the holiday spirit. The show's lively choreography, colorful costumes, and holiday songs are sure to put a smile on your face.
- **Holiday-Themed Snacks and Treats**: Enjoy a variety of

holiday-themed food available throughout the park, such as festive **sugar cookies**, **hot cocoa**, **gingerbread treats**, and **Grinch-themed snacks**. Be sure to try the Grinch-inspired **green desserts** to celebrate the season in style.

2. Winter Wonderland

Winter Wonderland at Universal Studios Hollywood transforms the park into a **festive winter paradise** with twinkling lights, towering Christmas trees, and holiday decorations. This enchanting experience provides a variety of family-friendly activities, perfect for creating lasting memories during the holiday season.

Event Dates:

- **When**: Winter Wonderland typically runs **from mid-November through early January**, overlapping with the Grinchmas celebrations. It's an excellent addition to the park's festive holiday lineup.

Tip: Double-check the park's schedule, as exact dates and times can vary each year.

Event Highlights:

- **Festive Lights and Decorations**: Throughout the park, you'll find stunning **holiday lights** adorning the buildings, streets, and trees. The **Upper Lot** and **Lower Lot** are both beautifully decorated, offering a perfect backdrop for photos. There's even a chance to stroll through **snow-covered areas** in the park to add a little extra winter magic to your day.
- **Ice Skating Rink (Seasonal)**: For an added layer of winter fun, Universal Studios

141

Hollywood often features a **temporary ice skating rink** in the park. It's a perfect spot for families to glide across the ice, all while surrounded by holiday cheer.

- o **Tip**: Ice skating can be popular during the holiday season, so check for any specific time slots to avoid waiting in line too long.
- **Holiday-Themed Entertainment**: In addition to Grinchmas, the Winter Wonderland experience also features various **holiday performances** throughout the park. Enjoy everything from **Christmas carolers** to live **musical numbers** celebrating the magic of the season.
- **Winter Photo Ops**: With all the holiday décor, there are plenty of **photo opportunities** scattered throughout the park. From Christmas trees and twinkling lights to snowy Whoville scenes, it's the perfect time to snap festive pictures with your loved ones.
- **Themed Holiday Treats**: During Winter Wonderland, you'll find a **variety of special seasonal treats** available at various food stalls and restaurants. Try a warm cup of **hot cocoa**, enjoy **seasonal desserts**, or indulge in a **holiday-themed churro** to satisfy your sweet tooth.

3. Other Limited-Time Experiences in 2025

In addition to Grinchmas and Winter Wonderland, Universal Studios Hollywood offers a variety of other limited-time experiences that can make your visit even more exciting. While exact events for 2025 are not yet confirmed, here are some recurring experiences you can expect:

A. Springtime Events

- **SpringFEST**: Universal may offer special spring-themed events with limited-time attractions, food, and shows to celebrate the season. Keep an eye out for these fun, family-friendly experiences.

B. Summer Nights

- **Summer Night Concert Series**: Universal Studios Hollywood often hosts outdoor concerts featuring live performances by popular artists, covering a range of genres. Enjoy music and dancing under the stars in the park's open-air spaces during summer nights.

C. Lunar New Year Celebrations

- **Lunar New Year** (usually in January or February) brings vibrant performances, special food, and limited-time merchandise celebrating Asian culture and traditions. Past celebrations have included **Dragon Dance performances**, **themed food stalls**, and **character meet-and-greets** with Mulan, Pooh, and friends.

D. Universal's Holiday Parade featuring Macy's

- **Holiday Parade**: The **Universal Studios Hollywood Parade** features massive balloons, floats, and performances with the larger-than-life character figures from the Macy's Thanksgiving Day Parade, making it a must-see during the holiday season.

Universal Studios Hollywood's **Grinchmas** and **Winter Wonderland** are just the beginning of the magical seasonal experiences awaiting you in 2025. Whether you're visiting for the **holiday cheer of Grinchmas**, enjoying a **snowy Winter Wonderland**, or taking part in other limited-time events like **Lunar New Year** or **Summer Nights**, the park offers something for everyone. Be sure to plan your visit during these special times to experience all the festive fun and make lasting memories with your loved ones.

CHAPTER 10

Accessibility and Inclusivity at Universal Studios Hollywood

Universal Studios Hollywood strives to make its attractions, services, and facilities accessible to all visitors, ensuring that everyone can enjoy the magic of the park. Whether you're visiting with mobility challenges, hearing impairments, or visual impairments, Universal provides a variety of services and accommodations to make your experience as comfortable and enjoyable as possible.

1. Wheelchair Accessibility Across the Park

Universal Studios Hollywood is committed to providing accessibility for guests with mobility disabilities. This includes wheelchair accessibility across all parts of the park, from rides to restrooms, dining areas, and more.

Wheelchair Rental:

- **Where to Rent Wheelchairs**:
    - **Wheelchairs** are available for rent at the **Guest Services** booth located at the park's main entrance. These are available on a **first-come, first-served basis** and are free of charge. A **$25 deposit** (refundable upon return) is required when renting a wheelchair.
    - **Electric Convenience Vehicles (ECVs)**: If you need a more mobile option, **ECVs** (scooters) are available for rent as well. The rental fee for an ECV is approximately **$75 per day**, with a **$25 deposit** required.
- **Wheelchair Accessibility on Attractions**:

- Most major rides and attractions are accessible to wheelchair users. However, some may require guests to transfer from their wheelchair to the ride vehicle, such as **The Simpsons Ride** or **Revenge of the Mummy**. Universal provides **assistive personnel** and signage to help guide you through the process.
- **Access Pass**: For guests who cannot transfer to a ride due to mobility impairments, the **Guest Relations** team can issue an **Access Pass**. This pass allows for easier access to rides and attractions without having to wait in standard lines. However, some attractions may have specific accommodations, so always check with Guest Services or the ride attendants.

Navigating the Park:

- **Ramp Accessibility**: Most of the park is equipped with **ramps** and **elevators** to ensure smooth access between levels. The **Upper Lot** and **Lower Lot** are connected by **elevators** and **wide ramps**, so guests in wheelchairs can easily move between these areas.
- **Accessible Restrooms**: Throughout the park, there are accessible restrooms designed for wheelchair users, typically located near major attractions, restaurants, and rest areas.
- **Parking**: Universal Studios Hollywood offers accessible parking spaces near the entrance of the parking structure. These spots are available on a first-come, first-served basis, so it's best to arrive early.

---

2. Services for Guests with Hearing or Visual Impairments

Universal Studios Hollywood provides several services and accommodations to assist guests with hearing or visual impairments, ensuring they can fully enjoy their visit.

A. Hearing Impairments

- **Assistive Listening Devices**:
  - **Assistive listening devices** are available for use in several venues, including shows and theaters. These devices amplify sound for guests who are deaf or hard of hearing, making it easier to hear the audio of live performances, pre-recorded audio, and sound effects.
  - **How to Get Them**: These devices can be requested at the **Guest Services** booth located at the entrance or at the theater hosting the show you plan to attend. They are provided free of charge but require a **valid ID** as a deposit.
- **Sign Language Interpretation**:
  - Universal Studios Hollywood may offer **sign language interpreters** for some live shows or special events, but this is typically available upon request. It's recommended to notify **Guest Services** in advance, as interpreter availability depends on the day's programming.
- **Closed Captioning**:
  - Many of Universal's **attractions** and **shows** offer **closed captioning** for video and audio-based content. The **Studio Tour** and other rides like **The Simpsons Ride** provide closed captioning via **video screens** for those who require them.
  - Guests can also request closed captioning devices for certain shows and attractions at **Guest Services**.
- **Visual and Auditory Notifications**:
  - For guests who are hard of hearing, some shows and attractions have **visual alerts** (flashing lights, screens) to signal important moments. Additionally, emergency procedures within the park often feature **visual cues** such as flashing lights for those who may not hear standard announcements.

B. Visual Impairments

- **Guides for Visually Impaired Guests**:
    - Universal Studios Hollywood offers **Braille guides** and **large print maps** to help guests with visual impairments navigate the park. These are available at **Guest Services** upon request.
- **Audio Descriptions**:
    - For certain attractions, **audio description** is available, which provides detailed narration of what's happening on-screen or around the guest. This is particularly helpful for attractions like **Universal's Studio Tour**, where guests can listen to audio descriptions while exploring the park's movie sets.
- **Orientation and Assistance**:
    - Guests with visual impairments who may need extra assistance navigating the park can request a **Guided Tour** or other support services. **Guest Services** can arrange for a park guide or other accommodations to help provide additional support, making it easier for you to get around the park.
- **Ride Accessibility**:
    - Some rides may have specific accommodations for visually impaired guests. For example, **interactive elements** on attractions like **The Simpsons Ride** or **King Kong 360 3D** may be described for guests who are blind or have low vision, allowing them to engage with the attraction.
- **Service Animals**:
    - Universal Studios Hollywood welcomes **service animals** that assist guests with visual impairments.

Service animals are allowed throughout the park, and special guidelines are provided to ensure a comfortable experience for both guests and animals.

o Universal offers **designated relief areas** for service animals, which are located in various parts of the park for easy access.

Additional General Services:

- **Tactile Maps**: Universal Studios Hollywood also offers **tactile maps** for visually impaired guests. These maps feature raised symbols and textures to help guests better understand the layout of the park.
- **Accessibility of Shows**: For many of the park's live shows and attractions, audio descriptions, captioning, and other accommodations are available, so be sure to check with **Guest Services** or inquire at the theater entrances to ensure you have the accommodations you need.

3. General Accessibility Tips:

- **Plan Ahead**: If you or a member of your party requires accessibility services or accommodations, it's always a good idea to **contact Guest Services in advance** or upon arrival to make sure you're aware of all the available options and services during your visit.
- **Visit Guest Services**: Universal Studios Hollywood's **Guest Services** team is happy to assist with any specific needs. Whether you need information on services for guests with disabilities or help navigating the park, they are the primary point of contact for accommodations.
- **Download the Universal Studios App**: The **Universal Studios Hollywood app** can also help you navigate the park with up-to-date information on accessibility features, wait times, show schedules, and more. It's a useful tool for staying informed during your visit.

Universal Studios Hollywood is dedicated to creating an inclusive environment for all guests, with extensive services and accommodations for individuals with mobility, hearing, and visual impairments. Whether you're renting a wheelchair, requesting an assistive listening device, or needing special assistance on a ride, the park ensures that everyone can experience the magic of its attractions. For guests with disabilities, planning ahead and utilizing the accessibility services available will ensure a smooth, enjoyable day at the park.

Sensory-Friendly Attractions and Quiet Zones at Universal Studios Hollywood

Universal Studios Hollywood is committed to providing an inclusive and accommodating environment for all guests, including those who may be sensitive to sensory stimuli. For individuals with sensory sensitivities or autism, the park offers a variety of **sensory-friendly attractions** and **quiet zones** to ensure a comfortable experience throughout your visit.

1. Sensory-Friendly Attractions
While Universal Studios Hollywood's rides and attractions are designed to entertain guests of all ages, some can be overwhelming for individuals with sensory sensitivities due to loud noises, sudden movements, or intense visual effects. To assist in creating a more comfortable experience, Universal offers some sensory-friendly alternatives.

A. Studio Tour

- **Why It's Sensory-Friendly**: The **Studio Tour** is one of Universal's most popular attractions, offering a behind-the-scenes look at famous film sets and iconic movie scenes. The tour provides a quieter, more relaxed environment with controlled lighting, low-volume sound effects, and relatively smooth motion.
- **How It Helps**: The tour is a **non-thrill** experience, offering a slower pace and plenty of breaks between the attractions. Guests with sensory sensitivities can enjoy the film sets without the intense stimuli present in some of the more high-octane rides.
- **Tips**: The Studio Tour is a great way to experience the magic of Universal Studios Hollywood without overwhelming sensory input. If you need to step away from the main attraction, there are calm areas within the tour route to take a break.

B. The Wizarding World of Harry Potter

- **Why It's Sensory-Friendly**: Although some parts of **The Wizarding World of Harry Potter** can be busy and crowded, the experience is largely immersive and sensory-friendly in certain areas. For example, **Hogsmeade** offers a more tranquil atmosphere, and the **Hogwarts Castle** provides quieter moments when you explore the shops and attractions in the area.
- **How It Helps**: The **Hogwarts Castle** attraction (specifically the **Flight of the Hippogriff**) is relatively calm with less intense motion or flashing lights compared to other thrilling rides. Additionally, guests can enjoy a more relaxed pace while exploring the **Hogwarts Castle**, **The Three Broomsticks**, and other quieter areas in the land.

C. Despicable Me: Minion Mayhem

- **Why It's Sensory-Friendly**: While this ride is an interactive experience, **Despicable Me: Minion Mayhem** has a relatively moderate level of sensory input, with its fun, family-friendly atmosphere and less-intense motion effects. It's also an excellent option for those who enjoy some motion but may find other rides too overwhelming.
- **How It Helps**: The ride uses screens and 3D effects rather than heavy physical motion or sound, making it a good choice for guests with sensory sensitivities.

D. Animal Actors Show

- **Why It's Sensory-Friendly**: The **Animal Actors Show** is a live performance that features trained animals demonstrating their skills in a variety of hilarious and cute stunts. The show has a lower level of sensory input and is free from sudden loud noises, fast movements, or flashing lights.
- **How It Helps**: This live show is a quieter, more relaxed option for guests who prefer a sensory-friendly environment. It's a fun, family-friendly experience with engaging animals and performers, without the intensity of some of the park's high-adrenaline rides.

2. Quiet Zones at Universal Studios Hollywood

To further assist guests who may need a calm space to decompress, Universal Studios Hollywood offers several **quiet zones** scattered throughout the park. These spaces are designed for guests who need a break from the hustle and bustle, providing a peaceful retreat to relax and recharge.

A. Guest Services and Accessibility Center

- **Location**: The **Guest Services** booth at the park entrance, located on the **Upper Lot**, offers information about accessibility services and quiet spaces. They also provide visitors with detailed information on how to navigate the park's sensory-friendly features.

- **Why It's a Quiet Zone**: The **Guest Services Center** offers a calming environment where visitors can take a break and speak to a team member about any needs or concerns regarding accessibility, sensory-friendly attractions, or quiet spaces.
- **What to Expect**: If you're feeling overwhelmed, the Guest Services area can provide helpful tips or a quiet corner to relax in. The staff can also assist with any sensory concerns and direct you to other peaceful areas within the park.

B. Lower Lot Quiet Zones

- **Location**: The **Lower Lot** of Universal Studios Hollywood, particularly near the **Jurassic World: The Ride** and **Transformers: The Ride 3D**, offers several secluded areas with benches and shaded spaces for guests to rest.
- **Why It's a Quiet Zone**: These areas are often less crowded compared to the **Upper Lot**, offering a peaceful environment away from the more chaotic areas of the park. They provide a chance to sit and relax in a quiet space.
- **What to Expect**: In these areas, you'll find benches, shaded spots, and peaceful surroundings to take a break from the busy areas of the park. This quiet zone is ideal for those needing a calm retreat.

C. The Wizarding World of Harry Potter: Shaded Areas and Benches

- **Location**: While the Wizarding World of Harry Potter can be crowded during peak hours, there are several **shaded areas** with **benches** scattered throughout Hogsmeade where guests can rest and enjoy a more peaceful environment.
- **Why It's a Quiet Zone**: The themed areas are designed to be immersive, but parts of Hogsmeade and the area around **Hogwarts Castle** are quieter and less crowded, especially

during the early morning hours or late in the afternoon when crowds are thinner.

- **What to Expect**: These spots provide a tranquil escape for those who need a break from sensory overload. You can relax while taking in the scenic views of the castle and Hogsmeade.

D. The Studio Tour Waiting Area

- **Location**: While waiting for the **Studio Tour**, you can often find quiet spaces in the **waiting area** near the ride entrance.
- **Why It's a Quiet Zone**: The area is typically less crowded, and the low noise levels in this section of the park offer a calm atmosphere to rest before embarking on the tour.
- **What to Expect**: There are benches where you can sit and relax while waiting for your tour, and the space is generally free from loud sounds or overwhelming stimuli.

3. Additional Tips for Managing Sensory Sensitivities

- **Plan Your Visit During Off-Peak Times**: To avoid large crowds and long wait times, consider visiting the park during off-peak seasons or weekdays when crowds are smaller. This will give you access to quieter areas and provide a more relaxed environment.
- **Use the Universal Studios App**: The official **Universal Studios Hollywood mobile app** offers detailed maps and wait times for all attractions. It's a helpful tool for planning your day and avoiding areas of high congestion, allowing you to stay in more serene parts of the park.
- **Stay Hydrated and Take Breaks**: If you start feeling overwhelmed, take advantage of the quiet zones and sensory-friendly attractions to rest and rehydrate. Staying hydrated can help you feel more comfortable, and stepping away from busy areas will give you the chance to recover.
- **Talk to Guest Services**: If you need further assistance or specific accommodations, don't hesitate to approach **Guest**

Services. They can provide helpful advice on managing sensory sensitivities, direct you to the best quiet zones, and even issue an **Access Pass** for easier access to attractions.

Universal Studios Hollywood offers a variety of **sensory-friendly attractions** and **quiet zones** to ensure that guests with sensory sensitivities can enjoy a more comfortable experience. From gentle attractions like the **Studio Tour** to peaceful areas around the park, there are plenty of options to create a personalized and stress-free visit. Be sure to make use of the quiet spaces and special accommodations to help manage sensory overload and ensure a fun, enjoyable time at the park for everyone.

Best Times to Visit Universal Studios Hollywood

Planning the perfect visit to Universal Studios Hollywood involves considering factors like crowd levels, weather, and ride wait times. By understanding the best times to visit, you can make the most of your experience and avoid long waits or crowds. Here's a detailed guide to help you navigate when to visit, based on crowd patterns, weather, and strategies for avoiding long lines.

1. Crowd Patterns Throughout the Year
Universal Studios Hollywood is a popular destination, and crowd levels can fluctuate depending on the time of year, school vacations, and local events. Understanding these patterns will help you plan your visit to avoid the busiest days.
A. Peak Seasons (High Crowds)
- **Summer (June - August)**:
    - **Why It's Busy**: School is out, and families flock to Universal Studios Hollywood during the summer vacation. The park can be packed with visitors,

especially on weekends and during holidays like **Fourth of July**.

- o **Crowd Impact**: Long wait times for popular rides, crowded walkways, and packed dining areas.
- o **Best for**: Families with children who can only visit during summer break. Be prepared for longer waits and higher ticket prices.

- **Holidays (Thanksgiving, Christmas, New Year's)**:
  - o **Why It's Busy**: The holiday season is one of the busiest times at Universal Studios Hollywood. Visitors come from all over the world to experience special holiday events like **Grinchmas** and the **Winter Wonderland**.
  - o **Crowd Impact**: Expect long lines, especially during **Christmas week** and **New Year's Eve**, along with crowded parking lots.
  - o **Best for**: Those who want to experience the festive atmosphere but should be ready for peak crowds and wait times.

- **Spring Break (March - April)**:
  - o **Why It's Busy**: Students are on vacation, leading to increased attendance. Popular rides like **Jurassic World: The Ride** and **Transformers: The Ride 3D** can have long lines.
  - o **Crowd Impact**: Busy but not as intense as summer or the holiday season. However, attractions can still be crowded, and ticket prices may be higher.
  - o **Best for**: Visitors who want to enjoy the park with slightly shorter waits than in summer, though still expect large crowds during peak days.

B. Off-Peak Seasons (Lower Crowds)

- **Winter (January - February)**:
  - **Why It's Less Crowded**: Post-holiday season means fewer tourists. Visitors who want to avoid the crowds will find this to be an ideal time to visit.
  - **Crowd Impact**: You'll find much shorter lines, more relaxed park experiences, and lower ticket prices.
  - **Best for**: Those who want to avoid long lines and crowds, but be mindful that some attractions may close for maintenance during this time.
- **Fall (September - Early November)**:
  - **Why It's Less Crowded**: Schools are in session, and families are less likely to visit. This is typically the best time for crowd-averse visitors.
  - **Crowd Impact**: Wait times are shorter, and the park is more spacious. The crowds are typically manageable, with only the occasional busy weekend.
  - **Best for**: Anyone looking for a quieter experience, especially those who want to take advantage of the park's seasonal events like **Halloween Horror Nights** (September to October).

C. Moderate Seasons (Average Crowds)

- **Late Spring (May)**:
  - **Why It's Moderate**: While schools are still in session, May is a transition month between spring break and summer vacation, meaning crowds are moderate.
  - **Crowd Impact**: Some rides will have moderate wait times, but it's generally not as packed as the summer or holiday seasons.
  - **Best for**: Those looking to avoid the summer crowds but still enjoy a lively atmosphere.

2. Weather Guide by Season

The weather at Universal Studios Hollywood can impact your experience, from ride operations to comfort levels. Here's a breakdown of what to expect during each season to help you plan accordingly.

A. Spring (March - May)

- **Weather**: Generally mild with temperatures ranging from **60°F (15°C)** to **75°F (24°C)**. Expect comfortable weather with occasional rain showers, especially in March and April.
- **What to Wear**: Light layers and comfortable shoes for walking. Bring a light jacket or sweater for cooler mornings and evenings.
- **Best Time for**: Enjoying moderate temperatures, but pack a rain jacket just in case.

B. Summer (June - August)

- **Weather**: Hot and dry, with temperatures often reaching **80°F (27°C)** to **90°F (32°C)**. It's common for Southern California to experience heatwaves, so prepare for high temperatures.
- **What to Wear**: Light clothing, sunscreen, sunglasses, and a hat. Stay hydrated and consider wearing a hat to protect from the sun.
- **Best Time for**: Visiting with kids who are on summer vacation, though be prepared for the heat and crowds.

C. Fall (September - November)

- **Weather**: Temperatures range from **65°F (18°C)** to **85°F (29°C)**. Fall in Southern California is typically mild, with dry weather and some cooler evenings.
- **What to Wear**: Light clothing during the day, but bring a sweater or jacket for the evening.
- **Best Time for**: Comfortable weather, making fall an ideal time to visit if you want to avoid the summer heat.

D. Winter (December - February)

- **Weather**: Cooler temperatures ranging from **50°F (10°C)** to **70°F (21°C)**. Winter is typically the coolest season, with some rainy days in December and January.
- **What to Wear**: Layered clothing, including a warm jacket or coat, especially in the evening. It can get chilly after the sun sets.
- **Best Time for**: Avoiding the summer heat and crowds. The festive atmosphere makes winter a charming time to visit, especially for **Grinchmas**.

3. Avoiding Long Lines: Strategies and Tools

Universal Studios Hollywood can get crowded, but with the right planning, you can minimize wait times and make the most of your visit.

A. Universal Express Pass

- **What It Is**: The **Universal Express Pass** allows you to skip the regular lines at most major attractions, which can be a huge time-saver during peak times.
- **How It Helps**: If you're visiting during a busy season, this pass lets you enjoy priority access to rides and shows, reducing the time spent waiting.
- **Best for**: Visitors who want to make the most of their day without waiting in long lines.

B. Single Rider Lines

- **What It Is**: Many rides, including **Transformers: The Ride 3D** and **Revenge of the Mummy**, offer **Single Rider Lines**. These lines are typically shorter and allow guests to fill in empty spots on ride vehicles.
- **How It Helps**: This is a great way to reduce wait times if you're okay with riding alone or with someone you don't know.

- **Best for**: Solo visitors or groups that don't mind splitting up on rides to save time.

C. Early Entry and Rope Drop

- **What It Is**: Arriving right when the park opens, or during **early entry hours** for guests with certain ticket types (like **VIP or hotel guests**), allows you to experience some of the most popular attractions with minimal wait.
- **How It Helps**: The first few hours of park operation are usually the least crowded, so you can hit the major rides early before the lines build up.
- **Best for**: Those who want to get on the most popular rides before the crowds flood in.

D. Check Wait Times and Plan Accordingly

- **What It Is**: The **Universal Studios Hollywood app** provides real-time wait times for all major attractions, allowing you to make informed decisions about which rides to visit first.
- **How It Helps**: By checking wait times and adjusting your itinerary based on the park's busiest and quietest times, you can avoid long waits.
- **Best for**: Guests who are flexible with their schedule and can adjust their plans to avoid high-wait attractions.

By considering crowd patterns, weather conditions, and utilizing time-saving tools like the **Universal Express Pass** and **Single Rider Lines**, you can optimize your visit to Universal Studios Hollywood. To avoid crowds, aim for **off-peak seasons** such as **winter** or **fall**, and be sure to plan ahead to make the most of your time in the park. Whether you want to enjoy a more relaxed experience with fewer crowds or take advantage of shorter lines with a bit of extra investment, this guide will help you have a smooth and enjoyable visit to the park.

CHAPTER 11

Accommodations Accessible at Universal Studios Hollywood

Universal Studios Hollywood offers a variety of accommodations for guests, ranging from official hotel options to nearby lodging. Whether you're looking for luxury, convenience, or budget-friendly options, there's something for every type of traveler.

1. Universal Studios Hollywood Hotels
A. Universal's Hard Rock Hotel

- **Type**: Luxury
- **Location**: Adjacent to the park, just a short walk to the entrance.
- **Key Features**:
  - Rock-and-roll-themed decor.
  - Exclusive **early park access** for hotel guests.
  - Outdoor pool and cabanas.
  - On-site dining options including **The Kitchen** (American cuisine).
  - Fitness center and arcade.
  - Modern amenities like free Wi-Fi, flat-screen TVs, and iPod docking stations.
  - Family-friendly accommodations with spacious rooms.

B. Universal's Loews Hollywood Hotel

- **Type**: Upscale
- **Location**: Located in the heart of Hollywood, approximately 10 minutes by car from Universal Studios Hollywood.
- **Key Features**:

- o Stunning views of the Hollywood Hills and the iconic **Hollywood Sign**.
- o Located near **Hollywood Boulevard**, perfect for exploring the city.
- o Poolside lounge area with a pool and hot tub.
- o **Room service** and on-site dining at **Preston's** restaurant.
- o **Universal Express Ride Access** and **early park entry** for guests.
- o Fitness center and modern room amenities including high-speed internet and large flat-screen TVs.
- o Pet-friendly accommodations.

2. Nearby Hotels
A. Hilton Garden Inn Los Angeles/Hollywood

- **Type**: Mid-range
- **Location**: A short drive (around 10 minutes) to Universal Studios Hollywood.
- **Key Features**:
  - o Comfortable and spacious rooms with modern furnishings.
  - o On-site dining at **The Garden Grille**.
  - o Outdoor pool and fitness center.
  - o Shuttle service available to **Universal Studios** (additional charge).
  - o Free Wi-Fi and business services for corporate travelers.
  - o Family-friendly amenities like cribs and rollaway beds.

B. Best Western Plus Hollywood Hills Hotel
- **Type**: Budget to Mid-range
- **Location**: Roughly 15 minutes by car from Universal Studios Hollywood.
- **Key Features**:
  - Affordable, comfortable rooms with basic amenities.
  - Outdoor pool and hot tub.
  - Free breakfast to start the day.
  - **Shuttle service** to Universal Studios Hollywood available (additional charge).
  - Close to **Hollywood Boulevard** and other local attractions.

C. The Garland
- **Type**: Boutique
- **Location**: Approximately 10 minutes by car from Universal Studios Hollywood.
- **Key Features**:
  - Retro-inspired boutique hotel with vibrant décor.
  - Spacious rooms and family-friendly suites.
  - Heated outdoor pool, hot tub, and garden courtyard.
  - **Shuttle service** to Universal Studios included.
  - **On-site restaurant** offering American fare at **The Front Yard**.
  - Pet-friendly accommodations.
  - Fitness center and free Wi-Fi.

3. Budget-Friendly Options
A. Motel 6 Hollywood
- **Type**: Budget
- **Location**: About 15-20 minutes by car from Universal Studios Hollywood.
- **Key Features**:
  - Affordable accommodations with simple, clean rooms.

163

- o Free Wi-Fi and cable TV.
- o Pet-friendly with affordable rates.
- o Convenient location close to major attractions and highways.
- o Outdoor pool for relaxation.

B. Super 8 by Wyndham North Hollywood
- **Type**: Budget
- **Location**: Approximately 10 minutes by car to Universal Studios Hollywood.
- **Key Features**:
  - o Budget-friendly, clean rooms with basic amenities.
  - o Complimentary breakfast.
  - o Free parking (a rare benefit in Los Angeles).
  - o Pool area for guests.
  - o Free Wi-Fi and TV with cable channels.

4. Extended Stay and Vacation Rentals
A. Extended Suites Los Angeles
- **Type**: Extended Stay
- **Location**: About 15 minutes by car from Universal Studios Hollywood.
- **Key Features**:
  - o Suites designed for extended stays with kitchenettes.
  - o Affordable rates for longer stays.
  - o Free Wi-Fi and on-site laundry facilities.
  - o Proximity to Universal Studios Hollywood and other attractions.

B. Airbnb and Vacation Rentals
- **Type**: Varies (Luxury, Mid-Range, or Budget)
- **Location**: Available in neighborhoods surrounding Universal Studios Hollywood such as **Hollywood**, **North Hollywood**, and **Studio City**.

- **Key Features**:
    - Private homes, apartments, or guesthouses with more flexibility for larger groups or families.
    - Full kitchens, multiple bedrooms, and homey atmospheres.
    - Price range and location flexibility based on budget.
    - Options for families, solo travelers, or those looking for a more personal experience.

5. Luxury Hotels Further Afield
A. The Hollywood Roosevelt
- **Type**: Luxury
- **Location**: About 15 minutes by car from Universal Studios Hollywood.
- **Key Features**:
    - Historic, glamorous hotel dating back to 1927.
    - Iconic locations like the **Tropicana Pool** and elegant dining at **The Spare Room**.
    - Spacious rooms with luxurious amenities and art deco style.
    - Close to the Hollywood Walk of Fame and major attractions.
    - Excellent for guests who want a lavish experience.

B. The Ritz-Carlton, Los Angeles
- **Type**: Luxury
- **Location**: Around 20 minutes from Universal Studios Hollywood.
- **Key Features**:
    - 5-star hotel with lavish rooms and top-tier services.
    - On-site fine dining and luxury amenities.
    - Rooftop pool with stunning views of the city.
    - Concierge services and upscale shopping nearby.

- Close to downtown LA, offering access to other attractions and events.

Whether you're looking for the convenience of staying right next to the park at **Universal's Hard Rock Hotel**, enjoying a boutique experience at **The Garland**, or opting for budget-friendly options like **Motel 6 Hollywood**, Universal Studios Hollywood and its surrounding areas offer a range of accommodations. Each option provides varying levels of luxury, amenities, and proximity to the park, ensuring you can find the perfect place to stay during your visit.

Nearby Accommodations: On-Site Hotel Options at Universal Studios Hollywood

Universal Studios Hollywood provides guests with a selection of on-site hotel options, offering both convenience and comfort for those looking to stay close to the park. Staying at these hotels means you'll be just steps away from the attractions, entertainment, and dining, making it easier to maximize your time at the park.

1. Universal's Hard Rock Hotel
Overview:
Universal's Hard Rock Hotel is the most iconic on-site hotel at Universal Studios Hollywood, blending the world of rock-and-roll with luxurious accommodations. It's located just a short walk from the park entrance, making it an ideal choice for visitors who want to stay close to the action while enjoying the comforts of a high-end hotel.
Key Features:
- **Proximity to the Park**: The hotel is located just steps from Universal Studios Hollywood, making it extremely convenient for guests to access the park and its attractions quickly.

- **Theme and Design**: The hotel features a rock-and-roll theme throughout, with memorabilia from famous musicians and vibrant décor inspired by classic rock.
- **Exclusive Benefits**:
  - **Early Park Admission**: Enjoy early access to select attractions before the general public, available to hotel guests on select days.
  - **Universal Express Unlimited**: Skip regular lines for rides and attractions (available for guests who book certain packages).
- **Dining Options**:
  - **The Kitchen**: A family-friendly restaurant offering all-day dining, including American favorites like burgers, sandwiches, and desserts.
  - **The Bar at The Hard Rock Hotel**: A lounge offering drinks and light bites with a relaxed atmosphere.
- **Amenities**:
  - Outdoor **heated pool** with private cabanas and a hot tub.
  - Fitness center with state-of-the-art equipment.
  - On-site **arcade** and entertainment options for children.
  - Free Wi-Fi throughout the hotel.
  - Pet-friendly accommodations available (with additional fees).
- **Rooms and Suites**:
  - Spacious rooms decorated with a rock-and-roll theme.
  - Rooms are equipped with flat-screen TVs, iPod docking stations, and mini-fridges.
  - Suites offer added space and luxurious amenities.

Best For:
- Music lovers, families, and anyone who wants to be right next to the park with easy access to both the attractions and high-end amenities.

2. Universal's Loews Hollywood Hotel
Overview:

Although not directly within the Universal Studios theme park, **Loews Hollywood Hotel** is one of the top on-site accommodations near the park, located about 10 minutes away by car. It is situated in the heart of Hollywood, making it perfect for those who want to combine their Universal Studios experience with the excitement of Hollywood.

Key Features:

- **Proximity to the Park**: While it's not right inside the park, the hotel is only a short drive or shuttle ride away from Universal Studios Hollywood, offering easy access to the park's attractions.
- **Views**: Stunning views of the **Hollywood Hills, Hollywood Sign**, and **TCL Chinese Theatre**.
- **Exclusive Benefits**:
  - **Early Park Admission** for Universal Studios Hollywood and access to select attractions.
- **Dining Options**:
  - **Preston's**: On-site restaurant offering modern American cuisine with both indoor and outdoor seating options.
  - **Loews Hollywood Bar**: A casual spot for drinks and light bites.
- **Amenities**:
  - Heated outdoor **pool** and **hot tub** with city views.
  - **Fitness center** with modern equipment.
  - On-site **concierge** services and travel planning assistance.
  - **Free Wi-Fi** and business services for corporate travelers.
- **Rooms and Suites**:

- o Stylish, spacious rooms with contemporary design and luxury touches.
- o Rooms feature modern amenities like flat-screen TVs, mini-fridges, and plush bedding.
- o Premium suites with separate living areas and larger layouts.

Best For:
- Visitors who want an upscale, modern hotel near Universal Studios, with the added bonus of being able to explore Hollywood.

3. Universal's Cabana Bay Beach Resort (Future Option)
Overview:
Scheduled to open as part of Universal's ongoing expansion plans in the future, **Universal's Cabana Bay Beach Resort** is designed to offer guests an affordable yet charming experience with a retro beachside theme. Though this hotel may not yet be available, it will provide another great option for visitors looking for themed accommodations near Universal Studios Hollywood.

Key Features (Expected):
- **Proximity to the Park**: Will be conveniently located within close proximity to the park, offering easy access to Universal Studios Hollywood.
- **Theme and Design**: Inspired by the mid-century modern style of classic beach resorts, it will feature bright, playful décor.
- **Dining Options**:
  - o Poolside dining with a focus on light meals, snacks, and family-friendly dining.
  - o Casual restaurants serving breakfast, lunch, and dinner with a relaxed, fun atmosphere.
- **Amenities**:
  - o Large outdoor pool with a lazy river and waterslides, offering a fun way to unwind after a day in the park.

- o Fitness center and family game rooms.
- o On-site shopping and recreational activities for guests of all ages.
- **Rooms and Suites**:
  - o Rooms with vintage-inspired furniture and colorful designs.
  - o Larger suites for families, with separate living areas and more space for relaxation.

Best For:
- Budget-conscious families who want a fun, retro resort experience while staying close to Universal Studios Hollywood.

4. Nearby Universal Studios Hollywood Hotels (Additional Options)

A. Sheraton Universal Hotel
- **Proximity to the Park**: Located about 1 mile from Universal Studios Hollywood, offering a short shuttle or drive to the park.
- **Key Features**:
  - o Recently renovated rooms and a stylish outdoor pool.
  - o On-site dining at **The California's Restaurant**.
  - o **Free shuttle service** to Universal Studios.

B. Hilton Los Angeles/Universal City
- **Proximity to the Park**: Just 0.5 miles from Universal Studios Hollywood, walking distance from the park.
- **Key Features**:
  - o Spacious rooms with modern amenities.
  - o Outdoor pool with views of Universal Studios.
  - o **Shuttle service** to Universal Studios and other local attractions.
  - o Fitness center and business services for travelers.

C. The Garland

- **Proximity to the Park**: Located just 2 miles from Universal Studios Hollywood.
- **Key Features**:
    - Retro, boutique hotel with a fun, casual vibe.
    - Heated pool, hot tub, and free shuttle service to Universal Studios.
    - Family-friendly rooms and on-site restaurant.

Staying at on-site accommodations near Universal Studios Hollywood gives you the convenience of easy park access, exclusive perks, and a wide range of options for various budgets. From the **Hard Rock Hotel** with its rock-and-roll theme to the more centrally located **Loews Hollywood Hotel**, each on-site option offers unique benefits for every type of traveler. Whether you're looking for luxury, family-friendly fun, or a budget-conscious stay, Universal Studios Hollywood has something to suit your needs.

Recommended Hotels Near Universal Studios Hollywood

If you're looking to stay close to Universal Studios Hollywood but prefer options that aren't directly on-site, there are several excellent hotels nearby, offering great value, comfort, and easy access to the park. List of top recommended hotels near Universal Studios Hollywood:

1. Hilton Los Angeles/Universal City
Overview:
This hotel is one of the closest to Universal Studios Hollywood, located just a half-mile away, making it one of the most convenient options for visitors. It offers a combination of comfort, luxury, and accessibility.
Key Features:
- **Proximity to Universal Studios**: 0.5 miles, within walking distance or a short shuttle ride.
- **On-Site Dining**: **The Lobby Bar** and **California's Restaurant** serve a variety of American dishes and cocktails.
- **Amenities**: Outdoor pool with views of the park, fitness center, business services, and meeting rooms.
- **Shuttle Service**: Offers a shuttle to Universal Studios Hollywood and other nearby attractions.
- **Family-Friendly**: Spacious rooms, some with panoramic views of the Hollywood Hills or Universal City.

Best For: Guests who want a high-quality, full-service hotel close to the park with luxury amenities.

2. Sheraton Universal Hotel

The Sheraton Universal Hotel is just one mile from Universal Studios Hollywood, and it offers a blend of convenience and comfort with its range of amenities and prime location.

Key Features:

- **Proximity to Universal Studios**: About 1 mile from Universal Studios Hollywood.
- **Shuttle Service**: Complimentary shuttle service to Universal Studios and nearby attractions.
- **On-Site Dining**: **The California's Restaurant** offers California cuisine, and there's also the **Universal Bar & Grill**.
- **Amenities**: Outdoor pool, fitness center, concierge services, and a business center.
- **Renovated Rooms**: Spacious and modern rooms with premium bedding, flat-screen TVs, and workstations.

Best For: Families and travelers looking for a comfortable stay with a free shuttle to the park.

3. The Garland

Overview:

Located just 2 miles from Universal Studios Hollywood, The Garland offers a retro-chic vibe with a relaxed atmosphere. It's a fantastic option for those who prefer a boutique hotel experience.

Key Features:

- **Proximity to Universal Studios**: 2 miles, with a free shuttle service to Universal Studios.
- **On-Site Dining**: **The Front Yard** offers American cuisine with a modern twist.
- **Amenities**: Outdoor heated pool, hot tub, fitness center, and family game room.
- **Family-Friendly**: Kid-friendly amenities like cribs, family rooms, and a welcoming environment for children.

- **Unique Design**: Mid-century modern design with colorful accents, offering a nostalgic feel.

Best For: Families and travelers who enjoy a quirky, comfortable hotel with a retro vibe and free shuttle service.

4. Hotel Amarano Burbank

Overview:

Located in Burbank, about 3 miles from Universal Studios Hollywood, Hotel Amarano is a luxury boutique hotel that offers a more serene, upscale experience while still being close to the park.

Key Features:

- **Proximity to Universal Studios**: Approximately 3 miles away, a short drive or shuttle ride.
- **On-Site Dining**: **The Grill Room** offers elegant dining with a focus on American fare.
- **Amenities**: Outdoor heated pool, fitness center, rooftop lounge, and complimentary car service within a 3-mile radius.
- **Luxury Rooms**: Stylish and comfortable rooms with custom furnishings, luxury linens, and premium toiletries.
- **Exclusive Perks**: Complimentary wine service in the evening.

Best For: Travelers seeking a quiet, luxurious boutique hotel with personalized service and proximity to Universal Studios.

5. Best Western Plus Hollywood Hills Hotel

Overview:

Located around 1.5 miles from Universal Studios Hollywood, this budget-friendly hotel offers a comfortable stay without breaking the bank. It's ideal for visitors who want good value and proximity to the park.

Key Features:

- **Proximity to Universal Studios**: 1.5 miles, a short drive or walk.
- **On-Site Dining**: Continental breakfast included, and there are plenty of nearby restaurants within walking distance.
- **Amenities**: Outdoor pool, fitness center, and free Wi-Fi.
- **Affordable Rates**: One of the most budget-friendly options for visitors staying close to Universal Studios Hollywood.
- **Rooms**: Clean, spacious rooms with basic amenities like flat-screen TVs and mini-fridges.

Best For: Budget-conscious travelers who still want a comfortable, convenient stay near Universal Studios Hollywood.

6. The Hollywood Roosevelt

Overview:
A historic hotel located on Hollywood Boulevard, just a short drive (about 3 miles) from Universal Studios Hollywood, The Hollywood Roosevelt is one of LA's most iconic hotels, offering luxury and old-school glamour.

Key Features:

- **Proximity to Universal Studios**: About 3 miles from the park, with easy access via car or taxi.
- **Historic Significance**: A famous hotel where the first Academy Awards were held, offering a blend of Hollywood history and modern luxury.
- **On-Site Dining**: **18 Thirty Lounge** for craft cocktails, and **The Public Kitchen & Bar** for American cuisine.
- **Amenities**: Outdoor pool, spa services, fitness center, and a beauty salon.
- **Rooms and Suites**: Luxurious rooms with a vintage Hollywood vibe, high-end furnishings, and modern amenities.

Best For: Travelers who want to experience the glamour of old Hollywood with a luxurious, historic stay while still being close to Universal Studios.

7. The Moment Hotel
Overview:

Located about 3 miles from Universal Studios Hollywood, The Moment Hotel is a chic boutique hotel offering modern amenities at an affordable price.

Key Features:

- **Proximity to Universal Studios**: 3 miles, a short drive or taxi ride away.
- **On-Site Dining: The Moment Café** offers casual dining with breakfast and light meals.
- **Amenities**: Rooftop bar with panoramic city views, fitness center, and free Wi-Fi.
- **Rooms**: Modern, well-appointed rooms with sleek décor, minibars, and flat-screen TVs.

Best For: Travelers looking for a stylish and affordable option with a modern flair, just a short drive from Universal Studios Hollywood.

8. Residence Inn by Marriott Los Angeles Burbank/Downtown
Overview:

This extended-stay hotel, located about 3 miles from Universal Studios Hollywood, is perfect for longer stays or families who need more space and amenities during their visit.

Key Features:

- **Proximity to Universal Studios**: 3 miles, with easy access to the park and other attractions in Burbank and Hollywood.
- **On-Site Dining**: Complimentary breakfast each morning and a **grocery delivery service** for those who prefer to cook in.

- **Amenities**: Outdoor pool, fitness center, and full kitchen facilities in the suites.
- **Family-Friendly**: Spacious suites with separate living areas, perfect for families or larger groups.

Best For: Families, extended stays, or anyone looking for a home-like experience near Universal Studios Hollywood.

These nearby hotels offer a variety of accommodations to suit different needs and budgets while being close to Universal Studios Hollywood. Whether you're looking for luxury, a boutique experience, or a budget-friendly stay, these options will provide easy access to the park and other local attractions. From the high-end amenities of **Hilton Los Angeles/Universal City** to the budget-conscious **Best Western Plus Hollywood Hills**, you'll find the perfect spot to rest and recharge after an exciting day at the park.

Transportation Options from Hotels to Universal Studios Hollywood

When staying near Universal Studios Hollywood, getting to and from the park is easy, with a variety of transportation options available. Whether you're staying in one of the on-site hotels or a nearby property, here are the main transportation choices to help you navigate your visit:

1. Walking Distance

Many hotels are located within walking distance of Universal Studios Hollywood, making it a convenient and simple option for guests staying close by. For those staying at hotels like **Hilton Los Angeles/Universal City** (0.5 miles away) or **Sheraton Universal Hotel** (1 mile away), walking to the park is often the quickest and most affordable method.

- **Average Walking Time**: 10–15 minutes from most nearby hotels.
- **Walkable Routes**: Most hotels near Universal Studios are connected by well-marked pedestrian paths that are safe and well-lit, offering a pleasant walk through the Universal City area.
- **Best For**: Guests who prefer a quick and simple journey with minimal hassle.

2. Shuttle Service

Many hotels near Universal Studios Hollywood offer **complimentary shuttle services** to and from the park, providing guests with a hassle-free transportation option. This is especially convenient for those who want to avoid the walk or need to get to the park quickly.

Hotels Offering Shuttle Service:

- **Sheraton Universal Hotel**: Offers a free shuttle service to Universal Studios Hollywood, making it an excellent option for guests looking for convenience.
- **Hilton Los Angeles/Universal City**: Provides a shuttle service to Universal Studios Hollywood, often included in the room rate or for a nominal fee.
- **The Garland**: Offers a free shuttle service to Universal Studios, making it a great option for families.
- **Service Frequency**: Shuttle services typically run every 15–30 minutes depending on the hotel and time of day.
- **Best For**: Guests who prefer to avoid the walk or don't want to

drive to the park. Shuttles are especially convenient for families or those traveling with large groups.

3. Public Transportation

If you prefer to use **public transportation**, Los Angeles offers various bus and subway routes that connect the Universal City area with other parts of the city, including **Hollywood** and **Downtown LA**.

Metro Red Line:

- **Proximity**: The **Universal City/Studio City Metro Station** is located just a short distance from the park entrance.
- **Routes**: The **Metro Red Line** is the easiest way to get from central Los Angeles to Universal Studios. It provides direct access to the **Universal City station**.

- **Service Hours**: The Metro Red Line operates daily from early morning to late night, making it a reliable option.
- **Cost**: The fare for the Metro Red Line is typically around $1.75 per ride.

Bus Services:

Several **Los Angeles Metro Bus** routes also pass through Universal City, providing an affordable public transportation option for visitors.

- **Bus Lines**: Look for bus routes 150, 155, and 488 that serve the Universal City area.
- **Cost**: Bus fares are also typically around $1.75 per ride.
- **Best For**: Budget-conscious travelers looking for affordable transportation options.

4. Taxis and Ride-Sharing Services

Taxis and **ride-sharing services** like **Uber** and **Lyft** are widely available in the Universal Studios Hollywood area. These services offer a more personalized and direct route to the park.

Taxis:

- **Availability**: Taxis are easily available from most hotels near Universal Studios. You can ask the front desk to arrange one, or you may be able to catch one from a designated taxi stand.
- **Cost**: A taxi ride from nearby hotels like the **Sheraton Universal** or **Hilton Los Angeles** can cost anywhere from $7–$15, depending on the distance and traffic conditions.

Ride-Sharing Services (Uber/Lyft):

- **Availability**: Ride-sharing services are readily available via apps, with pick-up locations at most hotels.
- **Cost**: A ride from hotels near Universal Studios typically costs between $5–$15, depending on traffic, the time of day, and the type of ride you select (e.g., UberX, UberXL, Lyft Standard, etc.).
- **Best For**: Those looking for a direct, convenient option to get to the park, especially if you're traveling with a group or have a lot of items with you.

5. Car Rental

For those who prefer the flexibility of having their own vehicle, **car rentals** are available at many hotels in the area or nearby rental locations. Car rentals are an option for those planning to visit multiple attractions around Los Angeles during their stay.

Rental Locations:

- Many rental car services are available at **Los Angeles**

International Airport
(LAX) or at car rental
companies in the
Hollywood area.

- **Hotel Locations**:
  Some hotels, like **The
  Garland** and **Hilton
  Los Angeles**, offer car
  rental services or
  partnerships with
  nearby rental agencies.

Parking:

- If you rent a car, you'll
  need to plan for
  parking fees at
  Universal Studios
  Hollywood. Parking
  costs can range from
  $25 to $50 per day,
  depending on the lot
  (general parking or
  preferred parking).
- **Valet Parking**: Valet
  parking is also
  available at many
  hotels near Universal
  Studios.
- **Best For**: Those who
  want the freedom to
  explore the city at their
  own pace or visit
  multiple attractions

outside of Universal
Studios Hollywood.

6. Private Car and Limousine Services

For those looking for luxury
and convenience, private car
or **limousine services** can be
arranged through hotels or
third-party services. These
services provide direct
transportation to Universal
Studios Hollywood in comfort
and style.

Services:

- **Private Sedans** and
  SUVs: Comfortable,
  private vehicles for
  you and your group.
- **Limousine**: For a
  more extravagant
  experience, you can
  opt for a limousine
  service to Universal
  Studios.

**Cost: Private car services
can range from $50 to $100+
depending on the vehicle
type, distance, and service
provider.**

- **Best For**: Luxury
  travelers or groups
  who want a

comfortable, private, and stylish way to get to Universal Studios.

7. Universal Studios Hollywood Parking Lot Shuttle

If you're driving to the park and need to park in one of the more distant lots, you can take advantage of the **Universal Studios Hollywood parking lot shuttles**. These shuttles are available to transport visitors from remote parking lots to the park entrance.

- **Shuttle Frequency**: Shuttles run frequently, so you'll never have to wait long.
- **Cost**: Parking costs generally range from **$25 to $50** per day, with preferred parking

being on the higher end of that scale.

- **Best For**: Visitors who prefer to drive but want to avoid long walks from parking lots.

Whether you prefer walking, using public transportation, or taking a shuttle, there are plenty of convenient transportation options available to get to Universal Studios Hollywood from nearby hotels. If you're staying at a nearby hotel, **shuttle services** and **walking** are the easiest ways to reach the park, while **ride-sharing services** and **public transportation** offer great alternatives for flexibility and convenience.

CHAPTER 12

Exploring Beyond the Park: Universal CityWalk – Shopping, Dining, and Entertainment

After a thrilling day inside Universal Studios Hollywood, you don't have to leave the fun behind. Just outside the park lies **Universal CityWalk**, a vibrant, dynamic entertainment district filled with everything from shopping to dining to live entertainment. It's the perfect way to extend your experience and continue enjoying the excitement of the area. Here's a detailed guide on what to expect when you explore **Universal CityWalk**.

1. Universal CityWalk

Universal CityWalk is an open-air complex located just steps away from Universal Studios Hollywood. Known for its lively atmosphere, eclectic mix of shops, restaurants, and entertainment venues, CityWalk is the ideal spot to unwind, eat, shop, and take in some of Los Angeles' best nightlife. The district covers **over 30 acres** and offers something for everyone, whether you're here to shop for exclusive merchandise, indulge in celebrity chef dining, or simply enjoy a stroll.

2. Shopping at Universal CityWalk

If you're looking to snag a souvenir or shop for something unique, CityWalk has plenty of options. Here are some of the top shopping experiences to enjoy:

Universal Studios Store
The flagship store of Universal CityWalk, the **Universal Studios Store**, is the go-to spot for all things

Universal. Here, you can find exclusive merchandise featuring your favorite movies, characters, and franchises from **Harry Potter** to **Minions** and **Jurassic Park**. From t-shirts to plush toys, and even collectible items, it's the perfect place to pick up a keepsake from your time at the park.

- **Highlights**: Exclusive movie-themed merchandise, collector's items, themed clothing, and toys.

The Harry Potter Store

For die-hard fans of the **Wizarding World**, the **Harry Potter Store** is a must-visit. This two-story store offers a wide range of Potter-themed products, including wands, scarves, robes, and magical artifacts. There's also a section dedicated to Hogwarts House merch, so you can pick up items that match your house's colors.

- **Highlights**: Authentic wands, Hogwarts robes, house-themed merchandise, magical stationery.

Blizzards and Arcade Games at the GameStop Store

For gamers, the **GameStop** store offers a variety of video games, collectibles, and gaming consoles. Whether you're looking for the latest releases or classic games, this store will keep you entertained. Plus, there are plenty of video game-themed merchandise and accessories to shop for.

- **Highlights**: Video games, gaming accessories, and collectibles.

Other Specialty Stores

- **Vans**: Shop for trendy footwear and apparel at the iconic Vans store, which is famous for its skate shoes and casual style.
- **Pandora**: Jewelry lovers will enjoy browsing the **Pandora** store, which offers a collection of

customizable charm bracelets, rings, and necklaces.

- **Lids**: A great stop for sports fans, Lids features a selection of hats and apparel for teams from across the U.S.

3. Dining at Universal CityWalk

CityWalk boasts a vibrant culinary scene, offering everything from quick bites to full-service dining, and featuring a variety of cuisines. Here are some of the top dining spots to check out:

Hard Rock Cafe

A classic stop for fans of rock 'n' roll, the **Hard Rock Cafe** offers a fun dining experience surrounded by iconic music memorabilia. The menu features classic American fare such as burgers, ribs, and salads. You can also enjoy a wide selection of cocktails and live music.

- **Highlights**: Burgers, sandwiches, signature cocktails, and rock memorabilia.

Bubba Gump Shrimp Co.

Inspired by the beloved film *Forrest Gump*, **Bubba Gump Shrimp Co.** offers seafood lovers a taste of shrimp, crab, and other delicious coastal dishes. The restaurant has a fun, laid-back vibe and is perfect for a family meal or casual dining.

- **Highlights**: Shrimp scampi, bucket of shrimp, seafood platters, and key lime pie.

The Toothsome Chocolate Emporium & Savory Feast Kitchen

For something unique, head to **Toothsome Chocolate Emporium**, where you can enjoy indulgent treats, decadent milkshakes, and even savory dishes. This steampunk-inspired restaurant is a favorite among visitors for both its food and whimsical atmosphere. Don't miss the over-the-top milkshakes, filled with chocolate, toppings, and even pastries.

- **Highlights**: Decadent milkshakes, chocolate-themed desserts, gourmet burgers, and pasta.

Panda Express

If you're looking for quick, affordable dining, **Panda Express** is a go-to spot for delicious Chinese food. Offering everything from Orange Chicken to Chow Mein, it's perfect for when you're on the go or craving some flavorful comfort food.

- **Highlights**: Orange chicken, Beijing beef, and fried rice.

Saddle Ranch Chop House

If you're in the mood for a Western-style dining experience, **Saddle Ranch Chop House** is a fun place to relax. Known for its giant cocktails, steaks, and a mechanical bull, it's a great spot for both families and groups of friends.

- **Highlights**: Ribs, steaks, giant cocktails, and an entertaining atmosphere.

Voodoo Doughnut

For those with a sweet tooth, **Voodoo Doughnut** is a must-try. This quirky doughnut shop offers unique and creative flavors, including the famous "Bacon Maple Bar" and other wacky, colorful doughnuts that make for a perfect Instagram photo.

- **Highlights**: Bacon maple bar, Voodoo doll doughnut, and other unusual flavors.

4. Entertainment at Universal CityWalk

In addition to shopping and dining, CityWalk is a prime location for entertainment, offering plenty of live shows, attractions, and even a movie theater. Here are the top entertainment options:

Universal Cinemas AMC

Catch the latest blockbuster films at the **Universal Cinemas AMC**, a state-of-the-art movie theater located at CityWalk. With IMAX and Dolby Cinema options, this theater offers an immersive movie-watching experience. You can enjoy a range of movie genres, from new releases to exclusive showings.

- **Highlights**: IMAX screenings, luxury seating, and a selection of snacks and beverages.

The Guitar Center Stage

For live music lovers, **The Guitar Center Stage** offers free live performances and concerts. You can enjoy a variety of musical acts, from local bands to well-known performers, depending on when you visit.

- **Highlights**: Free concerts, live performances, and a great atmosphere.

Billboard Radio Live

Head to **Billboard Radio Live** for live radio shows and performances by up-and-coming artists. It's the perfect spot to enjoy some live music and get a taste of the LA music scene.

- **Highlights**: Live performances, radio shows, and a lively ambiance.

5. Nightlife at Universal CityWalk

CityWalk doesn't stop when the sun sets. The nightlife here is lively, vibrant, and full of energy, with bars, clubs, and night-time entertainment that caters to all tastes.

The Red Piano Bar

For a more relaxed evening, head to **The Red Piano Bar**, a sophisticated spot where you can enjoy live piano music and cocktails. It's an elegant and laid-back venue that's perfect for winding down after a day at the park.

- **Highlights**: Live piano music, cocktails, and a classy ambiance.

Jillian's

If you're in the mood for a more energetic night out, **Jillian's** is a great option. Known for its arcade games, pool tables, and dance floor, it's perfect for those who want to combine nightlife with some fun activities.

- **Highlights**: Arcade games, pool tables, karaoke, and dancing.

Margaritaville

For a lively, island-inspired atmosphere, visit **Margaritaville**, where you can sip on tropical cocktails, enjoy tasty appetizers, and kick back to the sounds of beach-themed music. This is a great place to relax and enjoy the party vibe.

- **Highlights**: Margaritas, island-themed food, and a fun party atmosphere.

6. Events and Seasonal Activities

Throughout the year, Universal CityWalk hosts seasonal events and special activities, such as holiday festivities, live performances, and themed celebrations. During the holidays, you might find festive decorations, seasonal treats, and themed events like **Grinchmas** or **Halloween Horror Nights**.

Conclusion

Universal CityWalk is a vibrant and exciting destination that offers an entire world of entertainment just outside Universal Studios Hollywood. Whether you're shopping for unique souvenirs, enjoying a delicious meal, or unwinding with some nightlife, CityWalk ensures that your day doesn't have to end once you leave the park. It's the perfect place to continue the fun, relax, or discover new experiences, all while being just steps away from the iconic Universal Studios Hollywood.

CHAPTER 13

Nearby Los Angeles Attractions to Pair with Your Visit to Universal Studios Hollywood

While Universal Studios Hollywood offers an unforgettable experience on its own, Los Angeles is brimming with other world-class attractions and activities that you can easily pair with your visit. From art and culture to iconic landmarks and natural beauty, the city has something for everyone. Details to the top nearby attractions to explore before or after your time at Universal Studios Hollywood.

1. Griffith Observatory and Griffith Park

Located just a short drive from Universal Studios, **Griffith Observatory** offers stunning views of Los Angeles, including a direct line of sight to the **Hollywood Sign**. The observatory itself is a must-see for science and space enthusiasts, with interactive exhibits, telescopes, and informative shows. Griffith Park, one of the largest urban parks in the U.S., is also home to trails, picnic areas, and even a **Los Angeles Zoo**.

- **Highlights**: Spectacular city views, hiking trails, planetarium shows, the Hollywood Sign, and a variety of outdoor activities.
- **Distance from Universal Studios**: 10-15 minutes by car.

2. The Hollywood Walk of Fame

Just a short distance away from Universal Studios Hollywood, the **Hollywood Walk of Fame** is a historic sidewalk honoring more than 2,600 stars in entertainment. Located on **Hollywood Boulevard**, you can stroll along the sidewalk to see the names of your favorite celebrities, from actors to musicians, directors, and more. Nearby attractions include the **TCL Chinese Theatre**, **Hollywood Roosevelt Hotel**, and **Dolby Theatre**, home to the Academy Awards.

- **Highlights**: Star-studded sidewalk, celebrity handprints at TCL Chinese Theatre, and iconic landmarks.
- **Distance from Universal Studios**: About 5 minutes by car.

3. The Los Angeles County Museum of Art (LACMA)

For art lovers, the **Los Angeles County Museum of Art** (LACMA) is a must-visit. LACMA is the largest art museum in the western U.S. and features impressive collections of art from around the world, including contemporary, ancient, and modern art. One of its most famous installations is **Urban Light**, a collection of vintage street lamps that is iconic for photo ops.

- **Highlights**: Over 120,000 works of art, urban light installation, and rotating exhibits.
- **Distance from Universal Studios**: About 20-25 minutes by car.

4. The Getty Center

The **Getty Center** is a cultural haven, perched on a hilltop with breathtaking views of Los Angeles. The museum is known for its extensive art collections, including European paintings, sculptures, decorative arts, and manuscripts. Visitors can also explore beautiful gardens and architectural wonders, making it a peaceful and picturesque stop.

- **Highlights**: Art collections, architecture, gardens,

and panoramic views of the city.

- **Distance from Universal Studios**: Approximately 25-30 minutes by car.

5. Santa Monica Pier

If you're in the mood to hit the beach, head to **Santa Monica Pier**, which is about a 30-minute drive from Universal Studios. This iconic pier is home to an amusement park, aquarium, family-friendly restaurants, and an arcade. You can enjoy the sights and sounds of the beach, take a ride on the Ferris wheel, or walk along the scenic boardwalk.

- **Highlights**: Ferris wheel, beach access, aquarium, Pacific Park, and classic pier attractions.
- **Distance from Universal Studios**: 30-40 minutes by car.

6. The Natural History Museum of Los Angeles County

Located in **Exposition Park**, this museum is a great stop for families and anyone interested in learning more about the natural world. From dinosaur fossils to gems, minerals, and exhibits on ancient civilizations, the Natural History Museum is a fascinating experience that appeals to all ages.

- **Highlights**: Dinosaur skeletons, rare gems and minerals, and hands-on exhibits.
- **Distance from Universal Studios**: 20-25 minutes by car.

7. The California Science Center

Also located in **Exposition Park**, the **California Science Center** is a fun and educational attraction that's great for families. It houses interactive exhibits on science and technology, and it's also home to the Space Shuttle **Endeavour**. Visitors can engage with exhibits on ecosystems, physics, space exploration, and more.

- **Highlights**: The Space Shuttle Endeavour, interactive science exhibits, and IMAX theater.
- **Distance from Universal Studios**: About 20-25 minutes by car.

8. The Los Angeles Zoo and Botanical Gardens

Nestled within **Griffith Park**, the **Los Angeles Zoo** is home to over 1,100 animals from around the world. The zoo features themed exhibits like the **Rainforest of the Americas**, **Asian Elephant Habitat**, and **Africa's Wilds**. If you're a nature enthusiast or have kids with you, this is a fun stop after Universal Studios.

- **Highlights**: Animal exhibits, botanical gardens, and conservation efforts.
- **Distance from Universal Studios**: 15-20 minutes by car.

9. Venice Beach

For a quirky, laid-back experience, head to **Venice Beach**, located on the coast about 30 minutes from Universal Studios. Venice is famous for its colorful boardwalk, street performers, unique shops, and bustling atmosphere. You can also rent bikes or rollerblades and cruise along the beach path, or check out the famous **Venice Canals** for a scenic walk.

- **Highlights**: Beach activities, boardwalk, street performers, and the Venice Canals.
- **Distance from Universal Studios**: 30-40 minutes by car.

10. The Broad Museum

If you're a fan of contemporary art, you'll want to visit **The Broad Museum** in downtown Los Angeles. The museum is home to an impressive collection of modern and contemporary art, including works by Andy Warhol, Jeff Koons, and Roy Lichtenstein. Admission is free, but it's a good idea to reserve tickets in advance.

- **Highlights**: Contemporary art collection, free admission (reservations required), and architectural design.
- **Distance from Universal Studios**: About 20-25 minutes by car.

Los Angeles is a sprawling city with an incredible range of attractions, from cultural experiences to natural beauty and everything in between. Pair your visit to **Universal Studios Hollywood** with some of these nearby spots, and you'll have a truly memorable and diverse experience of the City of Angels. Whether you're interested in art, history, nature, or just a relaxing day at the beach, there's something for everyone in and around LA.

Budgeting Your Visit: Daily Expense Breakdown

Expense Category	Estimated Cost (Per Person)	Details/Notes
Tickets		
General Admission	$109 - $129	Prices depend on the date and availability. Tickets for one day of park entry.
Universal Express Pass	$179 - $249	Skip regular lines for select attractions. Prices vary by date and availability.
VIP Experience	$369 - $399	Includes front-of-line access, gourmet meals, and a personal tour guide.
Parking		
Regular Parking	$30 - $40	Standard parking for a single day.
Preferred Parking	$50 - $60	Closer parking to the park entrance.
Food & Beverages		
Quick Service Meals	$10 - $20	Fast food or casual dining options, like burgers, pizza, and salads.
Sit-Down Restaurant Meals	$20 - $50	Full-service dining at locations like the Three Broomsticks or Mel's Diner.
Snacks & Drinks	$5 - $15	Water, soda, popcorn, churros, or candy throughout the park.

Expense Category	Estimated Cost (Per Person)	Details/Notes
Souvenirs & Shopping		
Themed Souvenirs	$15 - $50	Wands, Minion plushies, t-shirts, and other park-exclusive merchandise.
Premium Souvenirs	$50 - $150	Limited-edition collectibles and high-end items.
Attractions & Experiences		
Studio Tour	Included in the ticket price	A must-do experience; included in the general admission or any package.
Special Tours (e.g., VIP Tour)	$399+	Includes all-day access with a personal guide, front-of-line access, and meals.
Transportation		
Uber/Lyft	$10 - $20 (one-way)	Estimated ride cost from hotels or other locations within the city.
Public Transportation (Metro)	$1.75 (per ride)	Metro lines and bus services for cheaper transportation options.
Miscellaneous		
Photo Services (if opted)	$20 - $50	Memory makers, photos, and other personal services.

Expense Category	Estimated Cost (Per Person)	Details/Notes
Mobile App (optional purchases)	$0 - $10	In-app purchases for virtual queue options or special park experiences.

Sample Daily Budget for One Adult

- **General Admission Ticket**: $129
- **Parking**: $40
- **Meals**: Quick Service Meals x 3 = $50
- **Souvenirs**: $25
- **Snacks/Drinks**: $10
- **Transportation**: $20 (Uber/Lyft)
- **Miscellaneous**: $10 (photo services)

Total Estimated Cost for the Day: $284

Sample Budget for a Family of Four (2 Adults, 2 Kids)

Expense Category	Estimated Cost (Family of 4)	Details/Notes
Tickets		
2 General Admission Tickets	$258 - $258	2 Adult tickets.
2 Child Tickets (Ages 3-9)	$216 - $258	2 Child tickets (discount for ages 3-9).
Parking		
Regular Parking	$40	
Food & Beverages		
Family Meals (4 meals)	$80 - $150	Combination of quick meals and sit-down restaurants.

Expense Category	Estimated Cost (Family of 4)	Details/Notes
Snacks & Drinks	$20	
Souvenirs	$50 - $100	Themed souvenirs and collectibles for the family.
Transportation		
Uber/Lyft	$40	Estimated round-trip for a family of four.

Total Estimated Cost for a Family of 4: $704 - $806

Additional Budget Tips:

- **Book in advance**: Some tickets, special experiences, and parking options can be cheaper if purchased ahead of time.
- **Bring snacks**: If you're traveling with younger kids or have dietary preferences, packing snacks and water can save money throughout the day.
- **Souvenir budget**: It's easy to get caught up in the excitement of the park, but setting a souvenir budget ahead of time can help you avoid impulse buys.
- **Consider multi-day tickets**: If you plan to visit the park for multiple days, purchasing multi-day tickets can be more economical than buying a one-day ticket per person.

By breaking down your daily expenses, you can better plan your visit to Universal Studios Hollywood and ensure you're not surprised by any hidden costs. Whether you're going solo, as a couple, or with your family, there are ways to manage your budget while making the most out of your day at the park!

Money-Saving Tips: Balancing Fun and Affordability at Universal Studios Hollywood

Visiting Universal Studios Hollywood can be an expensive experience, but with some thoughtful planning, you can enjoy all the fun the park has to offer while keeping your budget in check. Here are a variety of **money-saving tips** that will help you strike the perfect balance between having an amazing time and sticking to your budget.

1. Plan Your Visit During Off-Peak Times

One of the best ways to save money on your Universal Studios Hollywood trip is to visit during off-peak times. Crowd levels often influence ticket prices, and by avoiding peak seasons such as summer, major holidays, and weekends, you can not only get a more affordable ticket but also experience shorter lines and a less hectic atmosphere.

- **Best Times to Visit**: January to early February, mid-September through early November, weekdays in March and April, and early December before the holiday rush.

2. Buy Tickets in Advance and Online

Ticket prices for Universal Studios Hollywood can vary depending on the season, availability, and when you buy them. Purchasing your tickets **online and in advance** will typically save you money and time. Many online platforms or Universal's own website offer discounts for tickets bought ahead of time compared to purchasing at the gate.

- **Tip**: Look for promotions or bundle deals (like multi-day tickets) that can help reduce the cost per day.

3. Consider Multi-Day Passes

If you plan on spending more than one day at the park, purchasing a **multi-day pass** is one of the best ways to save per day. A **2-Day Ticket** or even a **3-Day Ticket** will often cost less than buying multiple single-day tickets, giving you extra time to explore the park without feeling rushed.

- **Tip**: If you're considering other nearby attractions (like Universal CityWalk), look for packages that combine tickets to the park and CityWalk or additional LA attractions.

4. Skip the Universal Express Pass

The **Universal Express Pass** allows you to skip the regular lines for certain attractions, but it can be quite pricey, especially if you're visiting during a non-peak time when lines are shorter. If you're not visiting during a particularly busy time, the extra cost may not be necessary.

- **Tip**: If you visit on an off-peak day, the lines should be manageable without the Express Pass, and you can use that money elsewhere.

5. Use Discounts and Promo Codes

Before purchasing your tickets or booking anything, check for **discounts or promo codes** that might be available. Sometimes, Universal offers seasonal discounts, and membership organizations like AAA or Costco also provide exclusive deals. You can also find discounts through sites like **Groupon** or **Travelocity**.

- **Tip**: Check for online reviews or social media groups for up-to-date discount codes and limited-time offers.

6. Bring Your Own Snacks and Water

Food and drinks within Universal Studios Hollywood

can be costly, especially if you're buying snacks throughout the day. Instead of purchasing snacks inside the park, **bring your own**. You can pack a small cooler or backpack with snacks like granola bars, fruits, sandwiches, and refillable water bottles. While larger meals may still need to be purchased inside, small snacks and drinks can help you save.

- **Tip**: Many amusement parks don't allow outside food or drinks to be brought into the park, but **Universal Studios Hollywood** does allow guests to bring in food for special dietary needs or small snacks. Just check the policy ahead of time.

7. Take Advantage of Free or Low-Cost Experiences

While some experiences at Universal Studios Hollywood come with an extra charge, there are plenty of **free or low-cost experiences** included with your ticket. For example:

- **The Studio Tour**: A must-do experience, this is included with general admission and offers an inside look at movie-making magic.
- **Live Shows**: Enjoy shows like **WaterWorld** and **The Special Effects Show**, which are included in your ticket and offer great entertainment without any additional cost.
- **Photo Ops**: Get plenty of great photos with costumed characters, which are typically free (although you can pay for professional photos).
- **Tip**: Utilize these included experiences to get the most out of your visit without extra cost.

8. Stick to Quick Service Dining

Sit-down meals at Universal Studios Hollywood can be quite expensive, with many themed restaurants charging high prices for both food and drinks. Instead, **opt for quick-service dining options**, which are usually more affordable but still offer a variety of delicious meals. You'll find casual dining options like burgers, pizza, and salads in various locations around the park.

- **Tip**: If you do want to splurge on a special meal, consider visiting for lunch, as many restaurants offer lower-priced lunch specials than their dinner options.

9. Avoid Buying Every Souvenir

While it's tempting to buy all the themed merchandise at Universal Studios Hollywood, souvenirs can quickly add up. **Set a souvenir budget** before you go, and stick to it. You can also look for cheaper alternatives like keychains, postcards, or other smaller keepsakes. If you're traveling with kids, let them pick one small item that fits your budget rather than buying several.

- **Tip**: Consider looking for Universal Studios Hollywood souvenirs at nearby stores outside the park, as prices can sometimes be lower.

10. Use Public Transportation or Ride Shares

Parking at Universal Studios Hollywood can be pricey, with regular parking starting at **$30** per day. **Public transportation** is a more affordable option if you're staying near a metro stop. Alternatively, **ride-sharing services** like Uber or Lyft can be a cheaper option for getting to the park from your hotel or other locations.

- **Tip**: Look for hotels near a metro station or

public transit options to save on parking and transportation costs.

11. Take Advantage of City Passes

If you plan on visiting multiple attractions in Los Angeles, consider purchasing a **City Pass** or **Go Los Angeles Card**. These passes bundle several attractions at a discounted price, which could help you save money if you plan to visit not only Universal Studios Hollywood but other top LA spots like the **Griffith Observatory, Los Angeles Zoo,** or **The Getty Center**.

- **Tip**: Check if your hotel or tour provider offers any discount passes or packages.

12. Free Parking After Hours

If you plan to visit **Universal CityWalk** after your day at the park, take advantage of **free parking** after 6 pm. This can save you quite a bit of money, especially if you just want to shop or enjoy dinner without returning to the main park.

Balancing fun and affordability at Universal Studios Hollywood is definitely achievable with a little planning. By visiting during off-peak times, booking your tickets in advance, skipping unnecessary extras like the Universal Express Pass, and taking advantage of free experiences and discounts, you can maximize the enjoyment of your trip while minimizing the impact on your wallet.

CHAPTER 14

Insider Tips and Hacks for Universal Studios Hollywood

Maximize Your Experience

Universal Studios Hollywood is full of exciting attractions, world-class shows, and hidden gems that can make your visit truly unforgettable. To help you make the most out of your time and money, here are some insider tips and hacks that will elevate your experience, including the **best seats for shows**, maximizing your **Universal Express Pass**, and some secret strategies known only to locals.

Best Seats for Shows and Attractions: Where to Sit for the Best View

When visiting a theme park, sometimes the little details—like the best seats for shows and rides—can make a big difference in your experience. Here are some top tips on where to sit to ensure the best views and the most immersive experiences:

1. WaterWorld: A Live Sea War Spectacular

This thrilling stunt show is one of the most popular in the park, and for good reason. To get the best views:

- **Best Seats**: Aim for the **center of the lower seating section** for an immersive experience. These seats provide the best overall view of the action without getting splashed too much.
- **Pro Tip**: If you're looking for a splash zone (for a fun water experience), choose seats in the **first few rows**. Be ready to get wet, though, so consider bringing a poncho!

2. The Special Effects Show

This show is a must-see for anyone interested in the behind-the-scenes magic of movie-making. To get the best view:

- **Best Seats**: The **center sections of the theater** offer the clearest view of the live demonstrations. These sections typically have less obstruction and give you a full view of the action on stage and on screen.
- **Pro Tip**: Arrive a little early to ensure you're seated in the **first 5-10 rows**. This allows you to get up close to the special effects and even interact with the performers.

3. The Wizarding World of Harry Potter

The Harry Potter area is a visual feast, but the right seating can make your experience even more magical. For rides like **Harry Potter and the Forbidden Journey**:

- **Best Seats**: The seats with the best views are usually **in the middle of the ride vehicle**, giving you the most balanced view of all the magical effects.
- **Pro Tip**: For the **Flight of the Hippogriff**, sit toward the **back** for a smoother ride and better views of the magical creatures.

Maximizing the Universal Express Pass: Skip the Lines Like a Pro

If you want to maximize your time in the park and minimize your wait times, the **Universal Express Pass** is a game changer. Here's how to get the most out of this upgrade:

1. Prioritize Popular Attractions

The Universal Express Pass allows you to skip regular lines for several attractions, but not all rides are equal. Some attractions tend to have much longer lines than others, so prioritize those that tend to be the busiest:

- **Must-Use Attractions**:
  - **Jurassic World: The Ride**
  - **Transformers: The Ride 3D**
  - **Revenge of the Mummy: The Ride**
  - **Harry Potter and the Forbidden Journey**

- These rides are the ones that most people gravitate toward, and skipping their lines will save you tons of time.

2. Use Your Express Pass in the Morning

Many guests don't arrive early, which means that the first few hours of the day offer the shortest lines. However, **with the Universal Express Pass**, you can skip the wait and enjoy your favorite rides in record time. Make sure you use the Express Pass early in the day for the best return on your investment.

3. Plan Your Route to Avoid Backtracking

Once you have the Universal Express Pass, it's important to map out your day so you're not running from one end of the park to the other. Plan a route that flows logically to reduce walking time and maximize your experience:

- **Pro Tip**: Start with the most popular attractions in the **Upper Lot** like **The Wizarding World of Harry Potter**, then head down to the **Lower Lot** to hit up **Jurassic World** and **Transformers**.

4. Don't Forget the Single Rider Line

Even with the Express Pass, you might find that some rides have very high demand. For these cases, use the **single rider line** as a backup. If you're okay with splitting up from your group, this line often moves even faster than the regular Express line and can get you on attractions in no time.

Secrets Only Locals Know: The Hidden Gems and Hacks You Won't Find in a Guidebook

Universal Studios Hollywood has some hidden gems and clever hacks that only locals or frequent visitors know. Here's your insider look at some of the best-kept secrets:

1. Get the Most Out of CityWalk

Universal CityWalk is a fantastic spot to enjoy shopping, dining, and entertainment—but locals know how to make the most of it:

- **Free Parking After 6 PM**: If you're planning to visit CityWalk but don't want to pay for parking, **park for free after 6 PM**. This is a great way to enjoy dinner, shopping, and entertainment without the added parking costs.
- **Less Crowded Times**: Visit CityWalk **before or after your park visit**, especially in the evening when crowds thin out, and you can enjoy a quieter experience.

2. Use the Universal Studios Hollywood Mobile App

One of the most useful tools for navigating the park is the **Universal Studios Hollywood mobile app**. This app lets you:

- See **wait times** for all rides in real-time
- Check **showtimes** for live events
- Locate **restaurants** and find **special deals**
- Purchase **tickets and Express Passes** directly from your phone
- **Pro Tip**: You can also use the app to place an order at some food stands, so you don't waste time waiting in line for snacks.

3. Take the Studio Tour Early

The **Studio Tour** is one of the park's best experiences, but it can get very crowded later in the day. Locals often recommend taking it first thing in the morning, before the crowds start to build. You'll get the best view of iconic sets and soundstages, and you may even get to see a live production in action.

4. Score Discounted Tickets and Packages

Locals know that there are always deals to be found for Universal Studios Hollywood:

- **Annual Passes**: If you plan to visit more than once in a year, the **annual pass** offers great perks, like discounts on food and merchandise and priority access to certain events.
- **Bundle Deals**: Look for bundles that combine tickets to **Universal Studios** and nearby attractions like **Universal CityWalk** or other Los Angeles hotspots. These can save you money if you plan to do more than just the park.

5. Watch for Secret Pop-Up Events

Universal Studios Hollywood occasionally hosts **secret pop-up events** or surprise character meet-and-greets. These are often not advertised and are exclusive to social media followers or guests who know where to look. For example, seasonal events like **Grinchmas** or surprise appearances from **Harry Potter characters** can provide unique experiences.

My Final Thoughts

By using these **insider tips and hacks**, you can truly elevate your Universal Studios Hollywood experience, whether you're navigating the crowds, making the most of your Universal Express Pass, or discovering hidden gems in the park. With a little insider knowledge, you can maximize fun while saving time and money, ensuring that your visit is not only memorable but also affordable.

Final Checklist for Your Visit to Universal Studios Hollywood

Before heading to Universal Studios Hollywood, having a **final checklist** will ensure that you're fully prepared and ready to make the most out of your visit. Whether it's what to pack, key things to know, or tips for a memorable experience, this guide will help you stay organized for an unforgettable day.

What to Pack for a Day at the Park

Packing efficiently for your day at the park will help you avoid unnecessary stress and ensure you have everything you need to enjoy your time. Here's a comprehensive list of items you'll want to pack:

1. Comfortable Clothing and Footwear

- **Comfortable Clothes**: You'll be walking, standing, and possibly waiting in line for extended periods, so choose **light, breathable clothing** that allows freedom of movement.
- **Comfy Shoes**: Wear **comfortable, closed-toed shoes** since you'll be doing a lot of walking. Sneakers or supportive sandals are ideal.

2. Sun Protection
- **Sunscreen**: Even on cloudy days, the sun can be strong in Los Angeles. Pack a **broad-spectrum sunscreen** and reapply throughout the day.
- **Hat**: A **hat** or **cap** can provide extra sun protection for your face.
- **Sunglasses**: Protect your eyes from the sun with **UV-protected sunglasses**.

3. Refillable Water Bottle
- Staying hydrated is essential, especially in the California heat. Pack a **refillable water bottle** and take advantage of water refill stations around the park to avoid purchasing expensive bottled water.

4. Snacks
- While you can buy food at Universal Studios Hollywood, **small snacks** like granola bars, fruit, or crackers can save you money and give you energy throughout the day.
- **Pro Tip**: Universal allows guests to bring in food for special dietary needs, so feel free to pack accordingly.

5. Phone and Charger
- You'll need your **phone** to check wait times, look up showtimes, and possibly take photos.
- **Portable charger**: The park offers charging stations, but it's always a good idea to bring a **portable charger** in case your phone battery runs low.

6. Poncho or Jacket

- Weather can be unpredictable, so pack a **light poncho** or **jacket**, especially if you plan to take the **Studio Tour** or go on **WaterWorld**, which can get you wet.

7. Backpack or Small Bag

- A **small, clear bag** is ideal to carry all your essentials. Avoid bringing large backpacks, as there are size restrictions for items inside the park.
- **Pro Tip**: A bag with multiple compartments will make it easier to organize and quickly access your items.

8. ID, Credit Cards, and Tickets

- Make sure you have your **ID**, **credit card**, and **park tickets** (either paper tickets or digital versions saved to your phone) readily available for admission.

9. Autograph Book (Optional)

- If you plan to meet characters, bring an **autograph book** for characters to sign. Alternatively, you can get a **photo with the characters** to remember the moment.

Key Things to Know Before You Go

Before you step into Universal Studios Hollywood, here are some **key things to know** to help make your day run smoothly:

1. Park Hours and Showtimes

- **Check Park Hours**: Universal Studios Hollywood has varying park hours depending on the day and season. Be sure to check the **park's schedule** to know what time the park opens and closes.
- **Showtimes**: Make a note of the **live showtimes** for attractions like **WaterWorld** or the **Special Effects Show**, as these are time-sensitive events.

2. Security Procedures

- All guests must go through **bag checks** and **metal detectors** at the entrance. Expect security lines, especially during peak times, so arrive early to avoid delays.

3. Plan Your Day with the App

- Download the **Universal Studios Hollywood mobile app** to get up-to-date information on **wait times, showtimes,** and **food options**. It also helps you navigate the park.

4. Accessibility Options

- Universal Studios Hollywood is committed to making the park accessible to all guests. If you or someone in your party has mobility challenges or other needs, check out the **Accessibility Guide** for information on **wheelchair rentals, guest services,** and **sensory-friendly zones**.

5. Universal Express Passes

- If you have a **Universal Express Pass**, use it strategically to skip the lines for popular attractions. Be sure to check **ride restrictions** for height or accessibility limitations before queuing up.

6. Plan for Meals

- There are a variety of food options throughout the park, ranging from quick bites to full-service dining. Consider **mobile food ordering** to save time and avoid waiting in line.

Tips for a Memorable Experience

Make your Universal Studios Hollywood visit extra special with these helpful tips:

1. Arrive Early

- Arriving at the park before it opens gives you a head start on the crowds. This will also allow you to hit the most popular attractions with shorter wait times.

2. Use Single Rider Lines

- If you're okay with splitting up from your group, make use of **single rider lines**. These lines are often much shorter, allowing you to get on rides faster.

3. Take Advantage of the Photo Opportunities

- Universal Studios Hollywood has plenty of photo spots, from **character meet-and-greets** to iconic set pieces. Don't forget to snap some pictures along the way, and check out the **PhotoPass** options to capture professional photos.

4. Stay Flexible

- While it's great to have a plan, staying flexible will help you manage unexpected changes in the day. For example, rides might close for maintenance or the weather could impact showtimes. Always have backup options.

5. Take Breaks

- The park is large, and you'll be doing a lot of walking. Schedule some downtime to rest, hydrate, and enjoy the atmosphere of **Universal CityWalk** or the **Studio Tour**.

6. Bring a Water Bottle and Stay Hydrated

- Los Angeles can get hot, especially in the summer months. Staying hydrated will help you maintain energy and prevent dehydration, especially when walking around all day.

7. Be Ready to Have Fun!

- Finally, **enjoy the experience**! Whether it's your first visit or your tenth, Universal Studios Hollywood is a place where fun and excitement are always just around the corner. Be sure to take in the sights, interact with characters, and enjoy everything the park has to offer!

By following this **final checklist** and preparing with key knowledge before you go, you'll ensure that your trip to Universal Studios Hollywood is smooth, memorable, and enjoyable. With the right planning, you can maximize your time in the park, save money, and make the most of every ride, show, and magical moment.

Frequently Asked Questions (FAQs) About Universal Studios Hollywood

Top Questions Visitors Ask

1. What time should I arrive at the park?

- **Best Answer**: Aim to arrive **before the park opens**. Early arrivals can take advantage of shorter lines, especially for the most popular attractions like **Harry Potter and the Forbidden Journey** and **Jurassic World: The Ride**. Plan to get there **30-45 minutes before opening time** to get through security and be among the first to enter.

2. Can I bring food into the park?

- **Best Answer**: **Generally, outside food and beverages are not allowed**, except for medical needs, baby food, or dietary restrictions. However, you can bring **small snacks** and a **refillable water bottle**. Universal allows food for babies, but it's always a good idea to check the official website for any updates on food policies before your visit.

3. What is the Universal Express Pass and is it worth it?

- **Best Answer**: The **Universal Express Pass** allows you to skip the regular lines for most attractions, saving time and making it easier to experience more in one day. It's **worth it** if you're visiting during peak times, such as holidays or weekends, or if you want to maximize your day with less waiting.

4. Are there any height or age restrictions for rides?

- **Best Answer**: Yes, there are height and age requirements for certain rides for safety reasons. For example, some attractions like **Jurassic World: The Ride** or **Revenge of the Mummy: The Ride** have specific height limits. Always check the ride requirements at the entrance or on the **Universal Studios mobile app** before you line up.

5. Are there any special events I should know about?

- **Best Answer**: Yes! Universal Studios Hollywood hosts a variety of **seasonal events** throughout the year, such as **Halloween Horror Nights**, **Grinchmas**, and **Lunar New Year** celebrations. It's a good idea to check the park's calendar to see if any special events align with your visit.

6. Can I meet characters in the park?

- **Best Answer**: Absolutely! **Character meet-and-greets** are a big part of the experience. You can meet characters from popular franchises like **Harry Potter**, **Minions**, **The Simpsons**, and more. Check the **schedule** or the **Universal Studios Hollywood app** for specific times and locations.

7. Is there a place to store my bags or personal items?

- **Best Answer**: Universal Studios Hollywood has **lockers** available for rent near the entrances of many attractions. This is particularly useful for storing items that aren't allowed on rides, like large bags or loose belongings.

8. Are there any discounts available for tickets or food?

- **Best Answer**: Yes, there are several ways to save money:
  - **Annual passes** offer discounts on tickets, food, and merchandise.
  - **Online ticket purchases** are typically cheaper than buying tickets at the gate.
  - Look for **special promotions** and **bundles** that include tickets for other local attractions or experiences.

Common Pitfalls and How to Avoid Them

1. Waiting in Long Lines Without a Plan

- **Pitfall**: One of the biggest challenges at Universal Studios Hollywood is the long lines, especially during peak times. Visitors without a plan may find themselves spending too much time waiting rather than experiencing the attractions.
- **How to Avoid**:
  - Use the **Universal Express Pass** to skip the regular lines.
  - Prioritize popular rides early in the day before the crowds arrive.
  - Download the **Universal Studios mobile app** to check real-time wait times and plan your route accordingly.

2. Underestimating the Size of the Park

- **Pitfall**: Universal Studios Hollywood is **larger than it may appear**. It's easy to get overwhelmed by the vastness of the park and feel rushed.
- **How to Avoid**:
  - Use the **park map** to plan your route ahead of time.
  - Consider taking **breaks** to rest, hydrate, and recharge.
  - Stay flexible, and be ready to change your plan if needed to avoid backtracking.

3. Missing Out on Live Shows

- **Pitfall**: The live shows at Universal Studios Hollywood, like **WaterWorld** and the **Special Effects Show**, are major highlights, but it's easy to miss them if you're focused only on the rides.
- **How to Avoid**:
  - Check the **showtimes** early in the day and **schedule** time for these shows.
  - Arrive early to get a good seat and ensure you're not late for popular shows.

o Use the **Universal Studios mobile app** to track showtimes in real-time.

4. Not Staying Hydrated or Taking Breaks

- **Pitfall**: Visitors often forget to stay hydrated or don't take enough breaks, which can lead to fatigue and irritability, especially in the hot weather.
- **How to Avoid**:
  o Pack a **refillable water bottle** and take advantage of free refill stations.
  o Take breaks at **shady spots**, **sit-down restaurants**, or **CityWalk** to relax and reenergize.
  o Listen to your body—take a breather when needed to avoid exhaustion.

5. Not Budgeting Enough for Meals and Souvenirs

- **Pitfall**: The costs of food and souvenirs can quickly add up, leaving you unprepared.
- **How to Avoid**:
  o Set a **budget** for food, souvenirs, and extra expenses ahead of time.
  o Look for **combo meal deals** or eat at **CityWalk** for cheaper food options.
  o If you plan to buy souvenirs, check out **exclusive deals** or discounts on the **Universal Studios Hollywood app**.

6. Not Taking Advantage of Single Rider Lines

- **Pitfall**: Long waits at popular attractions can take up a lot of time, especially if you're visiting during peak hours.
- **How to Avoid**:
  o If you're okay riding alone or splitting from your group, make use of the **single rider lines** to cut down on wait times.

7. Not Using the Universal Studios Hollywood App

- **Pitfall**: Visitors who don't use the **mobile app** might miss out on important information like wait times, showtimes, and dining options.
- **How to Avoid**:
  - o **Download** the **Universal Studios Hollywood app** before you go and familiarize yourself with its features.
  - o Use it to navigate the park, check real-time information, and even place food orders.

With these **top FAQs** and **common pitfalls** in mind, you'll be well-equipped to navigate Universal Studios Hollywood like a pro. Remember to plan ahead, stay flexible, and enjoy every moment of your visit. Whether it's your first time or your 10th, these tips will help you have a smoother, more enjoyable experience.

1-week itinerary

Day	Morning	Afternoon	Evening
Day 1	**Arrival & Check-In**: Settle into your hotel.	**Universal Studios Hollywood**: Explore the **Upper Lot** attractions like **The Wizarding World of Harry Potter** & **Despicable Me: Minion Mayhem**.	**CityWalk**: Dinner at **Vivo Italian Kitchen** & shopping.
Day 2	**Universal Studios Hollywood**: Visit the **Lower Lot** attractions like **Jurassic World: The Ride** & **Transformers: The Ride 3D**.	**Studio Tour**: Take the **Studio Tour** to see famous sets & enjoy **King Kong 360 3D & Fast & Furious Supercharged**.	**WaterWorld** Show & **The Simpsons Ride**. End with a stroll through **CityWalk** for dessert.
Day 3	**Nearby Attraction**: Visit **Griffith Observatory** for panoramic views of Los Angeles.	**Lunch at CityWalk**: Eat at **Hard Rock Café**. Then head to **Hollywood Walk of Fame**.	**Hollywood Sign** hike, followed by dinner at **Pine & Crane** for Taiwanese food.
Day 4	**Rest Day**: Relax by the pool at your hotel or visit **Universal CityWalk** for light shopping and dining.	**Explore Local Culture**: Head to **The Getty Center** for art exhibitions and gardens.	**Evening at The Grove**: Enjoy shopping and a movie.
	Universal Studios Hollywood: Experience the	**Visit a Museum**: Go to **The Museum of Contemporary Art**	**Grinchmas at Universal Studios** if

Day	Morning	Afternoon	Evening
Day 5	Special Effects Show and enjoy some family-friendly rides like **Secret Life of Pets: Off the Leash**.	(MOCA) or **LACMA** (Los Angeles County Museum of Art).	visiting during the holiday season or explore **CityWalk**.
Day 6	**Explore Beyond Universal**: Take a day trip to **Santa Monica Pier** and enjoy the beach.	**Santa Monica**: Enjoy the beach, pier, and local shopping.	**Dinner at The Lobster** overlooking the ocean.
Day 7	**Relaxing Morning**: Enjoy breakfast at **The Little Door** and relax before your departure.	**Visit a Nearby Theme Park**: If you have extra time, head to **Disneyland** or **Knott's Berry Farm** for a half-day visit.	**Departure**: Head to the airport for your flight back home.

This itinerary balances the excitement of Universal Studios Hollywood with time for exploring the surrounding areas, relaxing, and enjoying some local culture. You'll have the flexibility to adjust based on your pace, but this plan ensures you experience a little bit of everything!

3-day itinerary

Day	Morning	Afternoon	Evening
Day 1	**Arrival & Check-In**: Settle into your hotel.	**Universal Studios Hollywood**: Start with the **Upper Lot** attractions – **The Wizarding World of Harry Potter & Despicable Me: Minion Mayhem**.	**WaterWorld** Show & **The Simpsons Ride**. Afterward, explore **CityWalk** for dinner at **Vivo Italian Kitchen** and shopping.
Day 2	**Universal Studios Hollywood**: Spend the morning in the **Lower Lot** – enjoy **Jurassic World: The Ride, Transformers: The Ride 3D**, and **Revenge of the Mummy**.	**Studio Tour**: Take the iconic **Studio Tour** to explore movie sets and enjoy **King Kong 360 3D & Fast & Furious Supercharged**.	**Dinner at CityWalk** and enjoy a movie at the **Universal Cinema** or some late-night shopping.
Day 3	**Explore Nearby Attractions**: Visit **Griffith Observatory** or **Hollywood Walk of Fame**.	**Lunch at CityWalk**: Grab a bite at **Hard Rock Café** then head to **The Grove** for shopping.	**Evening Show**: Check out a show at **The Pantages Theatre** or end the day with a relaxing evening at **Santa Monica Pier**.

An Estimated budget for a 3-day Universal Studios Hollywood

Expense Category	Details	Estimated Cost (per person)	Total Estimated Cost (2 adults)
Accommodation	**Hotel** (3 nights at a mid-range hotel near Universal)	$150 - $300 per night	$450 - $900
Universal Studios Tickets	**General Admission** (1-day ticket)	$109 - $139 per ticket	$218 - $278
	Universal Express Pass (optional)	$179 - $249 per pass	$358 - $498
Food and Snacks	**Meals** (1 meal at the park per day)	$15 - $25 per meal	$90 - $150
	Snacks & Drinks (throughout the day)	$10 - $15	$60 - $90
Transportation	**Parking** (at Universal Studios)	$30 - $50 per day	$90 - $150
	Public Transport (or rideshare)	$20 - $40 (round trip)	$40 - $80
Souvenirs	**Shopping** (souvenirs, merchandise)	$20 - $100	$40 - $200
Nearby Attractions	**Griffith Observatory, The Grove, Santa Monica**	Free - $25 per attraction	$0 - $50

Expense Category	Details	Estimated Cost (per person)	Total Estimated Cost (2 adults)
Additional Activities	Special shows or events	$20 - $40 per person	$40 - $80
Miscellaneous	Tips, Miscellaneous purchases	$20 - $40	$40 - $80
TOTAL ESTIMATED COST	Overall Vacation Cost	$1,028 - $2,338	**$2,056 - $4,676**

Breakdown of Estimated Costs:

1. **Accommodation**: Costs vary depending on hotel rating, proximity to Universal, and time of year.
2. **Universal Studios Tickets**: Pricing depends on the type of ticket (general admission vs. Express Pass).
3. **Food and Snacks**: Meals can range from quick bites to full-service dining at the park. Budgeting $15-$25 per meal is realistic for moderate options.
4. **Transportation**: The cost of parking at Universal Studios Hollywood ranges from $30 to $50 per day. Alternatively, rideshare services or public transportation can reduce costs if parking fees are avoided.
5. **Souvenirs**: Depending on your shopping habits, this can vary widely.
6. **Nearby Attractions**: Many of Los Angeles' top attractions like Griffith Observatory are free, though some others (like **The Grove**) may require transportation or purchases.
7. **Additional Activities**: Special events and shows (like **Grinchmas** during the holidays) might carry additional costs.

This **estimated budget** should provide a good range of what you can expect to spend for a **3-day vacation** at Universal Studios Hollywood, considering all essential aspects of the trip.

Universal Studios Hollywood CHARACTERS

Franchise/Theme	Character(s)	Location/Appearance
The Wizarding World of Harry Potter	Harry Potter, Hermione Granger, Ron Weasley, Hogwarts Students, Wand Keepers	Hogsmeade Village
Despicable Me/Minions	Gru, Minions (Kevin, Stuart, Bob, etc.), Margo, Edith, Agnes	Near Super Silly Fun Land
The Simpsons	Homer Simpson, Marge Simpson, Bart Simpson, Lisa Simpson, Krusty the Clown	Springfield
DreamWorks Characters	Shrek, Fiona, Donkey (talking animatronic), Po (Kung Fu Panda), Poppy and Branch (Trolls)	DreamWorks Destination and roaming appearances
Transformers	Optimus Prime, Bumblebee, Megatron	Transformers: The Ride 3D area
Jurassic World	Blue the Velociraptor, Baby Dinosaur Encounters (Triceratops or other species)	Jurassic World area

Franchise/Theme	Character(s)	Location/Appearance
Illumination Entertainment	Snowball (The Secret Life of Pets), Max, Gidget, Duke	Secret Life of Pets: Off the Leash area
Universal Monsters	Frankenstein's Monster, Bride of Frankenstein, Dracula, The Mummy	Roaming the park during seasonal events or Halloween
SpongeBob SquarePants	SpongeBob, Patrick Star	Near Universal CityWalk or roaming appearances
Hello Kitty	Hello Kitty	Hello Kitty Shop in Universal Boulevard
Trolls	Poppy, Branch	Roaming near Universal Plaza
Scooby-Doo	Scooby-Doo, Shaggy, Velma, Daphne	Near the Mystery Machine
Mario & Luigi (Nintendo)	Mario, Luigi (during special events)	Universal Studios Special Appearances
Seasonal/Event Characters	The Grinch, Max the Dog (Grinchmas), Halloween Horror Characters	During seasonal events such as Grinchmas or HHN

This list provides a variety of characters that cater to different age groups and fandoms. It's worth checking with park staff for daily meet-and-greet schedules!

SCAN FOR YOUR MAP AND DIRECTIONS TO UNIVERSAL STUDIOS HOLLYWOOD

Made in the USA
Columbia, SC
28 March 2025